# JAPANESE MUSIC

GARLAND BIBLIOGRAPHIES IN
ETHNOMUSICOLOGY
(VOL. 2)

GARLAND REFERENCE LIBRARY
OF THE HUMANITIES
(VOL. 472)

# GARLAND BIBLIOGRAPHIES
# IN ETHNOMUSICOLOGY
*(Series editor: Fredric Lieberman)*

1. *Chinese Music: An Annotated Bibliography,*
   second edition, revised and enlarged
   by Fredric Lieberman

2. *Japanese Music: An Annotated Bibliography*
   by Gen'ichi Tsuge

# JAPANESE MUSIC
*An Annotated Bibliography*

Gen'ichi Tsuge

Garland Publishing, Inc. • New York & London
1986

**Library of Congress Cataloging-in-Publication Data**

Tsuge, Gen'ichi, 1937–
    Japanese music.

    (Garland bibliographies on ethnomusicology; 2)
(Garland reference library of the humanities ; v. 472)
    Includes indexes.
    1. Music—Japan—History and criticism—Bibliography.
I. Title.  II. Series.  III. Series: Garland reference
library of the humanities ; v. 472.
ML120.J3T8   1986   016.781752      83-49316
ISBN 0-8240-8995-2 (alk. paper)

Printed on acid-free, 250-year-life paper
Manufactured in the United States of America

To the memory of
*Fumio Koizumi*

# CONTENTS

# PREFACE

This annotated bibliography includes publications on
Japanese music in Western languages which appeared through
1983. Although its scope is limited primarily to publications
dealing with traditional Japanese music, some writings concerning dance, drama and/or performing arts of ritualistic
nature are inevitably included, as certain aspects of Japanese music are indeed inseparable from such areas.

Needless to say numerous valuable publications on
the subject exist in Japanese and other non-Western languages. Due to technical problems they have not been included
in this bibliography. The compiler, however, hopes to publish
another annotated bibliography dealing with those materials
as a separate volume in the near future.

Although intended to be as comprehensive as
possible, this bibliography is by no means exhaustive. Its
coverage is limited mainly to scholarly books, articles,
review essays, bibliographies and discographies. In general,
concert program notes, record album jacket notes, reviews and
journalistic writings of an introductory nature have been
excluded. Selection was based on significance as source
material, originality, accuracy of information and historical
value in Japanese music research. In this respect, translations of song-texts, libretti and synopses of dance-dramas
are included. Also collections of music in staff notation and
entries of an illustrative nature are included only if
accompanied by translations into Western languages or
romanized captions.

The compiler is not free from erroneous judgement
in selection and may be guilty of omitting a number of
valuable works. Corrections and/or additions from readers
will be greatly appreciated.

In regard to format, I have followed that of Chinese
Music by Fredric Lieberman, a counterpart in the present
Garland bibliography series. Each entry is followed by a
brief, critical annotation. The abbreviation "NE" (not
examined) indicates entries that I have not yet personally
examined; "AU" (author) indicates annotations provided by the
author of the given entry.

x

Special thanks to Fredric Lieberman who gave me the impetus to embark on compiling this volume, to Naoko Naitô and Masako Yokoi who undertook preliminary gathering of materials, to Mr. and Mrs. Henry Wakabayashi who kindly spent hours acquiring numerous hard-to-get materials from libraries in Washington D.C., and to Lynn Wakabayashi who assisted me in editing and proof-reading. The staff of the library of Kunitachi College of Music and of Tokyo Geijutsu Daigaku were extremely helpful in collecting and examining materials. Steven Nelson deserves special mention for his devoted assistance in the last stage of compiling this book. My sincere thanks are also due to Monica Bethe, Ury Eppstein, Kazuo Fukushima, Frank Hoff, Yoshihiko Tokumaru, Ruriko Uchida and Osamu Yamaguchi for their contributions of information and advice.

In matters of romanization of Japanese words, the Hepburn system is used with minor modifications. In entries, however, the original spelling is respected, needless to say. Surnames are spelled in capital letters. For Japanese names, the surname comes first, and the given name follows it, unless there is some established usage of the name in Western, that is reverse, order.

This book is dedicated to the memory of Fumio Koizumi who was first of all my teacher at Tokyo Geijutsu Daigaku, then colleague and friend at Wesleyan University, and now my late predecessor at Tokyo Geijutsu Daigaku.

G. T.

Tokyo
December 31, '84

# Japanese Music

# BIBLIOGRAPHY AND DISCOGRAPHY

1. BEARDSLEY, Richard K., John B. CORNELL, and Edward
   NORBECK, comps. Bibliographic Materials in the
   Japanese Language on Far Eastern Archeology and
   Ethnology. Ann Arbor: Univ. of Michigan, 1950.
   74p. (Bibliographic Series of the Center for
   Japanese Studies, The University of Michigan, 3).
   Contains many items dealing with folk and ritual
   singing and dancing of the Japanese and Ainu, as
   well as folklore studies of ethnic groups of
   Formosa, Micronesia, and Manchuria.

2. BRUNET, Jacques, ed. Oriental Music: A Selected Disco-
   graphy. New York: Foreign Area Materials Center,
   Univ. of the State of New York, State Education
   Department and the National Council of Associations
   for International Studies, 1971. iv, 100p.
   Japanese section includes 18 record albums released
   abroad as well as 22 Japanese albums, mostly sets of
   several discs, with annotations. Compiled for the
   International Institute for Comparative Music
   Studies and Documentation.

3. CROSSLEY-HOLLAND, Peter. "Oriental Music on the
   Gramophone." Music and Letters 40(1): 56-71,
   1959.
   Section 3 "Japan" includes a short list (five
   entries) with commentary which, however, has a
   number of misprints and is not extremely helpful.

4. ELISSEEV, Serge. "Notes bibliographiques sur la musique
   japonaise." In Essai sur les gammes japonaises
   by Noël Peri, p.63-70. Paris: Paul Geuthner, 1934.
   A fairly exhaustive bibliography on the subject;
   however information outdated.

5. ENDO Hiroshi. Bibliography of Oriental and Primitive
   Music. Tokyo: Nanki Music Library, 1929. viii,

1

62p.
Bibliography of books written in European languages
on non-Western music. No annotations. Contains 77
entries on Japanese music.

6. GERBOTH, Walter. An Index to Musical Festschriften and
Similar Publications. New York: W. W. Norton,
1909. ix, 188p.
Useful for searching for papers and articles on
Japanese music read and published in obscure
places.

7. _____. Music of East and Southeast Asia: A Selected
Bibliography of Books, Pamphlets, Articles and
Recordings. Albany: Univ. of the State of New
York, 1963. 23p.
Prepared for the non-specialist; geared to library
holdings in New York City areas. Contains 66 entries
concerning Japanese music, mostly in English, and 19
items of sound recordings.

8. GILLIS, Frank and Alan P. MERRIAM. Ethnomusicology and
Folk Music: An International Bibliography of
Dissertations and Theses. Middletown, CT: Wesleyan
Univ. Press, 1966. viii, 148p. (Special Series
in Ethnomusicology 1)
Contains 23 entries on Japanese music, somewhat
dated.

9. HAYASHIYA Tatsusaburô et al. "Historical Review of
Studies and References." Acta Asiatica 33:
74-90, 1977.
Annotated bibliography of Japanese language publications in the field of Japanese performing arts.
Divided into six sections according to historical
period.

10. HICKERSON, Joseph C. et al. "Current Bibliography and
Discography." Ethnomusicology 1-25, 1953-83
(current).
Extensive coverage of contemporary materials.

11. HOWLEY, F. "Some Recent Books on Nô." Monumenta
Nipponica 2(1): 293-300, 1939.
Bibliographical guide to Japanese studies on
nô, introducing Utaibon 'Omokage' by Mikami
(1937), Nôgaku shiryô Vols. 1 & 2 (1931-32),
and Zeami buyô tokuhon by Fujikage (1938).

12. INADA, Hide I. Bibliography of Translations Made from
    the Japanese into Western Languages. Tokyo: Sophia
    Univ. 1971. vi, 112p.
    Annotated bibliography of translations made during
    the period from the 16th century to 1912. Includes
    source materials concerning drama, folklore, histo-
    ry, mythology, and literature, as well as items on
    music.

13. ISHII Taeko. A Bibliography of Traditional Japanese
    Music in European Languages since 1950. Tokyo:
    Kunitachi Music College Library, 1978. 10p.
    Contains 213 entries. No annotation, no index.

14. JAPAN P.E.N. CLUB. Japanese Literature in European
    Languages: A Bibliography.Tokyo: Japan P.E.N.
    Club, 1961. xii, 98p.
    Gives title and Japanese author's name in both
    roman letters and Japanese characters. No annota-
    tion. Chapter III, "Classical Theater" includes
    literature on and translations of nô, kyôgen
    and kabuki plays.

15. _____. Japanese Literature in European Languages: A
    Bibliography (Supplement). Tokyo: Japan P.E.N.
    Club, 1964. iv, 8p.

16. KIMBALL, James and Gen'ichi TSUGE. Selective
    Bibliography of Japanese Music. Middletown, CT:
    Wesleyan Univ. Music Library, 1972. 6p.
    Classified bibliography of works in Western
    languages and Japanese. Contains 42 entries with
    annotation. Prepared primarily for librarians and
    students in the World Music Program.

17. KNOSP, Gaston. "Bibliographia Musicae Exotica." Revue
    musicale de la Société internationale de la
    Musique, Supplement. November 1910. 19p.
    The section Japon (p.5-8) includes 149 items,
    mostly in European languages. No annotation.

18. KOIZUMI Fumio. "Annotated Bibliography of Japanese
    Music." Ongaku Gaku 9: 55-64, 1963.
    Selected bibliography of works written in Japanese
    about traditional Japanese music. The first section
    deals with works on "Japanese Music in General"
    only. The remaining 10 sections were not completed.

19. KOKUSAI BUNKA SHINKOKAI. K.B.S. Bibliography of Standard Reference Books for Japanese Studies with Descriptive Notes. Vol. 7(B): Theatre, Dance and Music. Tokyo: Kokusai Bunka Shinkokai [The Society for International Cultural Relations], 1960. 182p. One of a series of classified and annotated bibliographies of standard reference books in Japanese. The section on music contains 103 entries which were published by the end of 1959. As an appendix, a brief list of selected works in Western languages, on Japanese drama, dance and music, is added.

20. _____. K.B.S. Bibliographical Register of Important Works Written in Japan on Japan and the Far East, Published during the Year 1932. Tokyo: Kokusai Bunka Shinkokai, 1937. vii, 166p. Entries on music p.86–94. Bibliography, including occasional annotations, of works in the Japanese language published in 1932. The section "Arts and Crafts" includes 53 entries on music, 4 on dance, and 20 on theater.

21. KUBOTA Satoko. "A Guide to the Basic Literature and Records for Research in Jiuta and Sokyoku." Trans. by Yamaguchi Osamu. Hogaku 1(1): 93–112, 1983. Well-organized listing with partial annotation of basic bibliographical and discographical items necessary for research on the genres jiuta and sôkyoku.

22. KUNST, Jaap. Ethnomusicology 3rd ed. The Hague: Nijhoff, 1959. x, 303p. Includes an extensive bibliography of ethnomusicological literature with over 4500 entries (93 entries on Japanese music). Somewhat dated.

23. _____. Supplement to the Third Edition of Ethnomusicology. The Hague: Nijhoff, 1960. vii, 45p. Adds 11 entries on Japanese music.

24. LAADE, Wolfgang. Gegenwartsfragen der Musik in Afrika und Asien: Eine grundlegende Bibliographie. Baden-Baden: Verlag Valentin Koerner, 1971. 110p. Lists 92 books and articles concerning Japanese music written in Western languages and introduces 35 periodicals in Japanese dealing with various kinds of music. An occasional brief annotation.

25. _____. Neue Musik in Afrika, Asien und Ozeanien: Disko-
graphie und historisch-stilistischer Überblick.
Heidelberg [privately printed], 1971. 463p.
Discography includes a total of 84 items for Japan
(p.27-29, 36-39), and commentary (p.188-228) deals
largely with recent developments in koto music
and contemporary Japanese music, and introduces a
fairly large number of composers.

26. MALM, William P. "Notes on Bibliographies on Japanese
Materials Dealing with Ethnomusicology." Ethno-
musicology 7(1): 39-40, 1963.
Introduction to four bibliographies.

27. _____. "Recent Recordings of Japanese Music: A Record
Review Essay." Ethnomusicology 11(1): 97-106,
1967.
Introduction and critical review of 18 record albums
of traditional Japanese music.

28. _____. "Special Bibliography: A Bibliography of Japanese
Magazines and Music." Ethnomusicology 3(2): 76-
80, 1959.
Introduction to commercial music magazines and
journals of various academic societies dealing with
the performing arts. Includes 25 entries, all in the
Japanese language. Contains some factual mistakes.

29. MATSUI Masao et al, eds. An Annotated Bibliography:
Japanese Performing Arts. Honolulu: Center for
Asian and Pacific Studies, Univ. of Hawaii, 1981.
318p.
Description of the holdings in the Japanese performing arts of the Thomas Hale Hamilton Library, Univ.
of Hawaii at Manoa. Contains 1020 items written in
Japanese; includes musical scores, collections of
song-texts, drama texts and stage scripts.

30. _____. Ryukyu: An Annotated Bibliography. Honolulu:
Center for Asian and Pacific Studies, Univ. of
Hawaii, 1981. 345p.
Catalog of the holdings on Ryukyu studies of the
Thomas Hale Hamilton Library, Univ. of Hawaii at
Manoa. The sections of Fine and Performing Arts and
Literature contain over 50 items concerning Okinawan
dance, song and music, all written in Japanese.

31. MATSUSHITA Hitoshi and YOSHINO Yoshiko. "Bibliography and

Discography." In Musical Voices of Asia [Report of ATPA 1978], p.345–81. Tokyo: Japan Foundation, 1980.
Contains 100 annotated items on Japanese music, focusing on books and articles dealing with folk songs, nô, shinnai, gidayû, koto and Buddhist music, in both Japanese and European languages. Also includes 50 record albums of the above-mentioned genres.

32. MINEGISHI Yuki. Discography of Japanese Traditional Music. Tokyo: Japan Foundation, 1980. 56p.
Contains a listing of 673 albums released during the period 1976–80. With introductory notes and index to original Japanese titles.

33. PURCELL, William L. "A Discography of Oriental Music. Part One: China, Korea and Japan." The American Record Guide 26(1): 8–11; 56–60, September 1959.
Includes 18 albums, with a short outline of traditional Japanese music and musical instruments.

34. SAKANISHI Shio. "Books on East Asiatic Music in the Library of Congress (Printed before 1800) II. Works in Japanese." In The Library of Congress Catalogue of Early Books on Music (Supplement), p.132–33. Compiled by Hazel Bartlett. Washington, D. C.: Library of Congress, 1944.
Extremely short (nine entries) annotated catalogue of early printed works in Japanese held in the Library of Congress. Includes material on gagaku, nô, and jôruri.

35. SCHMIEDER, Wolfgang. Bibliographie des Musikschrifttums. Leipzig & Frankfurt A.M.: Hofmeister, 1950–current.
Continuing series of annual publications.

36. SHULMAN, Frank J. Doctoral Dissertations on Japan and Korea, 1969–1974. Ann Arbor: Univ. of Microfilms International, 1976. 78p.
Supplement to Entry 37.

37. _____. Japan and Korea: An Annotated Bibliography of Doctoral Dissertations in Western Languages, 1877–1969. Chicago: American Library Association, 1970. xix, 340p.
The sections "Music," "Theatrical Arts," and

"History" include a number of doctoral dissertations
dealing with traditional Japanese music and other
performing arts.

38. SIEFFERT, René. "Bibliographie du théâtre japonais."
Bullentin de la Maison Franco-Japonaise, n.s. 3:
1-116, 1953.
Consists of two bibliographies: the first lists 543
Japanese books and periodicals with annotation (in
French) on theater, music and dance; the second
lists 140 works in European languages.

39. _____. "Etudes d'ethnographie japonaise." Bulletin de
la Maison Franco-Japonaise, n.s. 2: 7-110, 1952.
Contains a bibliography of ethnographic studies of
Japan, listing 378 entries with annotations (in
French). Section III (Divertissements) includes 16
items written in Japanese concerning music, dance,
and theater.

40. SILBERMAN, Bernard S. Japan and Korea: A Critical
Bibliography. Tucson, AZ: Univ. of Arizona Press,
1962. xiv, 120p. Section on "Japanese Art" includes
literature on nō theater, kyōgen, kabuki,
jōruri, and music.

41. TYRRELL, John and Rosemary WISE, A Guide to International Congress Reports in Musicology 1900-1975.
New York: Garland Publishing Inc., 1979. xiii, 353p.
Contains the titles of some 35 papers on Japanese
music, presented at various international congresses
in musicology during the last three quarters of a
century.

42. WATERHOUSE, David. "Hōgaku Preserved: A Select List of
Long-Playing Records Issued by Japanese Companies of
the National Music of Japan. " Recorded Sound
33: 383-402, January 1969.
Discography based on catalogues issued by seven
major Japanese record companies in 1966-68. Includes
1406 records, index, and glossary. All records are
LP, 33 1/3 rpm. Includes all classical genres as
well as some popular categories, such as ryū-
kōka, dōyō, rōkyoku, and even rakugo.

43. _____. "Hōgaku Preserved II : A Second Select List of
Long-Playing Records Issued by Japanese Record
Companies of the National Music of Japan."

Recorded Sound 57-58: 408-26, January-April
1975.
Discography listing 2009 records from 1973
catalogues of five Japanese record companies.
Includes an introductory survey of the history of
recorded sound in Japan.

44. WATERMAN, Richard A., William LICHTENWANGER, Virginia H.
HERRMAN, Horace I. POLEMAN, and Cecil HOBBS.
"Bibliography of Asiatic Musics." Notes 2nd s.
7(2): 266-79, 1950; 8(2): 328-29, 1951.
Listing of 314 entries on Japanese music, with
occasional annotations. A source containing a
surprising amount of material for its date.

45. _____. "Survey of Recordings of Asiatic Music in the
United States, 1950-51." Notes 2nd s. 8(4):
683-91, 1951.
15th installment of the "Bibliography of Asiatic
Musics." Lists 72 record collections (private,
public, institutional) with an index of contents,
divided according to ethnic group.

46. WATSUJI Tetsurô et al. A Bibliography of Represent-
ative Writings on Japanese Culture and Science.
Tokyo: Cultural Affairs Division, Office of Public
Relations, Foreign Office, 1947.
Material in Japanese on music and drama p.39-42.

47. YAMAGUCHI Osamu. "Bibliography." In Asian Musics in an
Asian Perspective [Report of ATPA 1976], p.339-64.
Tokyo: Japan Foundation, 1977.
Selected bibliography with annotations in the field
of ethnomusicology, and the musics of Southeast Asia
and Japan.

48. YOSHIZAKI Yasuhiro. Studies in Japanese Literature and
Language: A Bibliography of English Materials.
Tokyo: Nichigai Associates, Inc., 1979. 451p.
The section on "General Studies of Drama" includes
many works in English on bunraku, kabuki,
and nô, as well as traditional Japanese music
and musical instruments.

# DIRECTORIES AND PERIODICALS

49. BRIEGLEB, Ann. Directory of Ethnomusicological Sound
    Recording Collections in the U.S. and Canada. Ann
    Arbor, MI: Society for Ethnomusicology, n.d. [SEM
    Special Series 2] 46p.
    Includes 11 collections that contain sound record-
    ings of Japanese music.

50. JAPANESE NATIONAL COMMITTEE OF THE INTERNATIONAL MUSIC
    COUNCIL. Japanese Music Organizations 1. Tokyo:
    Japanese National Committee of the IMC, 1979. iii,
    67p.
    Directory of music agencies, associations, organized
    societies and performing bodies, based on the music
    annual, Ongaku Shiryô 1978.

51. LICHTENWANGER, William, Dale HIGBEE, Cynthia A. HOOVER,
    and Phillip T. YOUNG. A Survey of Musical Instru-
    ment Collections in the United States and Canada.
    Ann Arbor, MI: Music Library Association, 1974. xi,
    137p.
    List includes 20 collections that contain Japanese
    instruments.

52. SIDDONS, James. "Directory for Japan." In Directory of
    Music Research Libraries 4, p.61-164. Ed. by Rita
    Benton. Kassel: Bärenreiter, 1979 [RISM Publication
    Ser. C].
    Introduction and guide to Japanese libraries, the
    Japanese language and its romanization system, music
    research organizations as well as a list of general
    music literature (176 items both in Japanese and
    Western languages), and a directory of libraries
    that hold music materials (138 entries).

53. _____. "A Librarian's Guide to Musical Japan." Fontes
    Artis Musicae 24(2): 59-68, 1977.
    General remarks on Japanese musical life and its

relation to the West, historically important music
collections in Japan, as well as useful information
about Japanese books and related matters.

\* \* \* \* \* \* \* \* \* \* \*

54. Asian Music 1(1)-15(1), 1968-83 (current).
    Journal of the Society for Asian Music. Contains
    several articles on Japanese music as well as book
    and record reviews.

55. Ethnomusicology 1-27(3), 1953-83 (current).
    Journal of the Society for Ethnomusicology. Contains
    the largest number of scholarly articles concerning
    Japanese music of any English journal. Book reviews
    and record reviews deal occasionally with Japanese
    materials.

56. Gagaku Kai 1-58, 1949-83 (current).
    Journal of the Ono Gagaku Kai, a private gagaku
    study group. Recent issues contain several articles
    in English with Japanese translation.

57. Hogaku 1(1)-1(2), 1983 (current).
    Journal published semi-annually by the Traditional
    Japanese Music Society, a project of the Music
    Department of the Graduate Center of the City
    University of New York. Includes articles on
    Japanese music both technical and general in nature.

58. Journal of Asian Studies 1(1)-43, 1941-83 (current).
    Journal of the American Association of Asian
    Studies. Every September issue contains a
    comprehensive listing of new books and periodical
    literature. Published until 1956 (v.15) under the
    title The Far Eastern Quarterly.

59. Jahrbuch für musikalische Volks- und Völkerkunde 1-
    10, 1963-82. (Publication occasionally suspended.)
    Yearbook for studies in folk music and ethno-
    musicology. Limited number of contributions on
    Japanese music.

60. Monumenta Nipponica 1-38(4), 1938-83 (current)

Periodical devoted to Japanese studies, published by
Sophia Univ., Tokyo. The most scholarly magazine
dealing with Japanese culture in English. Oriented
toward literature; however, it contains occasional
articles on Japanese music, dance and drama and
translation of texts.

61. Music Index 1-35(12), 1949-83 (current).
    Monthly publication with annual cumulations. The
    sections "Far East" and "Japan" contain indexes of
    selected music periodicals.

62. Musica Asiatica 1-3, 1977-81 (current).
    An occasional periodical edited by Laurence Picken,
    and published by Cambridge Univ. Press. Devoted
    to historical musicology and organology of Asia.
    Contains several articles dealing with Japanese
    music.

63. Ongaku Gaku 1-29(3), 1955-83 (current).
    Journal of Ongaku Gakkai (the Japanese Musicological
    Society). Devoted to articles most of which are
    written in Japanese. Though basically oriented
    towards European musicology, includes occasional
    articles on Japanese music as well as other
    non-Western musics. Every article has a brief
    summary in either English, French, or German.

64. RILM Abstracts of Music Literature 1-12, 1967-83
    (current).
    Quarterly journal published by the International
    RILM Center, New York (Barry S. Brook, Editor-
    in-Chief). Contains abstracts of significant liter-
    ature on music of the world. Section of "Ethno-
    musicology" includes abstracts and titles of works
    on Japanese music.

65. Selected Reports in Ethnomusicology 1(1)-6, 1966-83
    (current).
    Formerly a publication of the Institute of
    Ethnomusicology of UCLA, and currently published by
    the Department of Music. Contains occasional
    research papers on Japanese music.

66. Tôyô Ongaku Kenkyû 1-48, 1936-83 (current).
    Journal of the Tôyô Ongaku Gakkai (Society for
    Research in Asiatic Music). Devoted mostly to
    scholarly articles on traditional Japanese and Asian

musics written in Japanese. Has some articles
written in European languages. Each article is
generally accompanied by a brief English summary.

67. World of Music 1-25(3), 1959-83 (current).
    Journal of the International Institute for
    for Comparative Music and Documentation, Berlin, in
    association with the IMC, UNESCO. Contains some
    articles concerning Japanese music and musical
    instruments. Scholarly but introductory in nature.
    Articles written in English, with French and German
    summaries.

68. Yearbook for Traditional Music 13-15, 1981-83
    (current), which is the continuation of the
    Yearbook of the International Folk Music Council
    1-12, 1969-80.
    Journal published annually by the International
    Council for Traditional Music (the former Inter-
    national Folk Music Council), a member organization
    of IMC, under the auspices of UNESCO. Contains some
    articles, far fewer than desired, on Japanese music,
    as well as book and record reviews.

* * * * * * * * * *

# BOOKS AND ARTICLES ON JAPANESE MUSIC

69. ABRAHAM, Otto and Erich M. von HORNBOSTEL. "Studien über das Tonsystem und die Musik der Japaner." Sammelbände der Internationalen Musikgesellschaft 4: 302-60, 1902-3. [Reprinted in Hornbostel Opera Omnia 1. Ed. by Klaus Wachsmann, Dieter Christensen, and Hans-Peter Reinecke. The Hague: Martinus Nijhoff, 1975. p.1-84.]
Pioneer work in the literature of comparative musicology concerning Japanese music. Deals with tone system, music theory, as well as practical aspects such as status of musicians, teaching, and theater. Appendix contains seven transcriptions.

70. ACKERMANN, Peter. Yamada Kengyô Untersuchungen zu Person und Wirken des Yamada-Koto Schule. Doctoral dissertation, Musikwissenschaftliches Institut, Univ. Basel, 1975. 219p., music.
Study of the music of Yamada Kengyô, the founder of the Yamada school of sôkyoku, dealing with the history, the music itself, and the relationship between text and music. Pieces dealt with in analytical terms include 13 traditional Yamada school pieces (9 by Yamada Kengyô), 2 Meiji-period Yamada school pieces, and 2 Ikuta school pieces for contrast.

71. ADDIS, Stephen. "Shichigenkin." In Kodansha Encyclopedia of Japan 7:87, 1983.
Short note on the musical instrument kin (Chinese qin) and its history in Japan.

72. _____. Uragami Gyokudô: The Complete Literati Artist. Doctoral dissertation, Univ. of Michigan, 1977. 707p.
Study of Urakami Gyokudô (1745-1820), as a musician, poet, calligrapher, and painter.

73. ADRIAANSZ, Willem. Introduction to Shamisen Kumiuta.

13

14

Buren: Frits Knuf, 1978. 127p.
Introduction to the genre shamisen kumiuta,
with a brief history and analysis (Pt 1), and an
anthology of shamisen kumiuta in Western staff
notation which contains seven pieces (Pt 2).

74. _____. "A Japanese Procrustean Bed: A Study of the
Development of Danmono." Journal of the
American Musicological Society 23(1): 26-60,
Spring 1970.
Analysis of danmono pieces of the koto
repertoire with a hypothesis concerning the origin
of danmono.

75. _____. 'Koto.' [Part 2 of §IV. Instruments and Their
Music] Sub-entry of the article "Japan." In New
Grove Dictionary of Music and Musicians 9: 526-32.
Ed. by Stanley Sadie. London: Macmillan, 1980.
Fairly detailed survey of the history and musical
forms of koto music that developed in the Edo
period.

76. _____. The Kumiuta and Danmono Traditions of Japanese
Koto Music. Berkeley & Los Angeles: Univ. of
California Press, 1973. xii, 493p.
Based on the doctoral dissertation, The Kumiuta
... Music, submitted to the Univ. of California,
Los Angeles, 1965. Contents: Pt. 1: Introduction to
the History of Koto Music, the Instruments, Scales
and Tunings, Notation, and Playing Techniques; Pt.
2: Danmono: the First Dan, the Later Dan, Other
Considerations; Pt. 3: Fuki, the First Kumiuta in
Hira-Jôshi, Kumiuta in Other Chôshi, the Vocal
Part; Pt. 4: Transcriptions of Selected Kumiuta and
Danmono following the tradition of the Ikuta-ryû
in Kyoto.

77. _____. "Letter to the Editor." Ethnomusicology 12
(1): 166-71, 1968.
Reply to the comments of Kikkawa and Holvik on
Adriaansz's "Research into the Chronology of
Danmono."

78. _____. "Midare: A Study of Its Historic Development."
In Nihon ongaku to sono shûhen [Festschrift
Professor Kikkawa Eishi], p.9-54. Ed. by Koizumi
Fumio, Hoshi Akira and Yamaguchi Osamu. Tokyo:
Ongaku no Tomo Sha, 1973.

Study based on the formal analysis of six extant
versions of Midare, one of the "multimovement
compositions" for koto solo, known as danmono.

79. _____. "Music and Tradition of the Edo Period." World
of Music 20(3): 69-75, 1978. With summaries in
French and German.
Brief survey of musical traditions of the Edo period
(1600-1860's). From a lecture delivered in the 1974
Musicultura at Breukelen, Holland.

80. _____. "On the Evolution of the Classic Repertoire of
the Koto," Proceedings of the Centennial Workshop
on Ethnomusicology (held at the University of
British Columbia, Vancouver, June 19-23, 1967),
p.68-78. Edited by Peter Crossley-Holland.
Vancouver: Government of the Province of British
Columbia, 1968.
Analysis of early koto danmono pieces (such as
Rinzetsu and Sugagaki) with an argument that
Midare-rinzetsu is not the work of Yatsuhashi
Kengyô.

81. _____. "Research into the Chronology of Danmono."
Ethnomusicology 11(1): 25-53, 1967.
Proposition for a chronology of the danmono
pieces based on stylistic evidence.

82. _____. "Rôsai." Ethnomusicology 3(1): 101-23, 1969.
Discussion of rôsai-bushi, a popular early
17th-century vocal form, with a comparison of the
structures of three extant pieces, Rôsai
(kumiuta for shamisen), Kumoi-rôsai
and Shin kumoi-rôsai (quasi-kumiuta pieces
for koto).

83. _____. "The Yatsuhashi-Ryû: A Seventeenth-Century
School of Koto Music." Acta Musicologica 43
(1-2): 55-93, 1971.
Introductory study of the Yatsuhashi school of
koto music and its repertory, with comparisons
of a piece common to the Tsukushi-goto, Yatsuhashi-
ryû, and Ikuta-ryû repertories.

84. AIZAWA Mutuo. "The Musical Taste of School Children."
Tôhoku Psychologica Folia 6(3): 111-26, 1938.
1931 questionnaire survey of Japanese school-
children's song preferences. Analysis included.

16

85. AKIYAMA Kuniharu. "Japan." In Dictionary of Contemporary Music, p.364-67. Ed. by John Vinton. New York: E.P. Dutton, 1971.
Historical review of Western music in Japan since the Meiji Restoration in 1868. Enumerates important composers who contributed to development of contemporary Japanese music up to the end of the 1960's.

86. ALEXANDER, Sister Mary. "Shômyô...Buddhist Chant." Geijutsu to shimpi [Ars et mystica] 14: 48-55, 1964; 15: 52-57, 1965; 16: 65-70, 1967; 18: 51-56, 1971; 19: 94-107, 1973.
Historical outline of the traditional Buddhist chant of Japan.

87. AMBESI, A.C. and MATSUSCITA Scin-ici [MATSUSHITA Shin'ichi]. "Giappone (Nihon, Nippon)." In Enciclopedia della musica 2: 308-10. Milano: Ricordi, 1964.
General survey of Japanese music, briefly describing scales and modes, history, and composers of modern Japan.

88. ANDÔ Tsuruo. Bunraku: the Puppet Theater. Translated by Don Kenny. Introduction by Charles J. Dunn. New York & Tokyo: Walker/ Wetherhill, 1970. 222p.
Generously illustrated introductory study of bunraku, centered around a historical account of the development and transmission of the art.

89. ANDÔ Yoshinori. "Structure and Acoustical Properties of a Chikuzen-Biwa." In Preservation and Development of the Traditional Performing Arts [Proceedings of ISCRCP 1980], p.163-79. Tokyo: Tokyo National Research Institute of Cultural Properties, 1981.
Pioneer work investigating the acoustical features of the chikuzen-biwa.

90. ANDÔ Yoshinori and SAGARA Taeko. "Pitch Intonation of Koto-Music." Oto to shisaku: Nomura Yosio Sensei kanreki kinen ronbun shû [Festschrift Professor Yosio F. Nomura], p.25-39. Tokyo: Ongaku no Tomo Sha, 1969.
Report of a series of experiments in measuring pitches used on the koto by five noted performers while playing fragments of Rokudan.

91. Anonymous. "Asagao (Morning-Glory), Translated from the 17th Century Japanese." Japan Magazine 2: 411-13; 470-73, 1911.
Translation of the story of Keisei tsukushi no tsumagoto, a kabuki play by Chikamatsu Tokuzō, generally known as Asagao nikki.

92. _____. [FUNAZAKI Hisashi]. "Gagaku: The Thousand-Year Tradition." The East 2(5): 9-18, June 1976. music, photos.
Lavishly illustrated introduction for foreigners to Japanese court music and dance. Tōgi Masatarô, a renowned court musician, and his family are featured in the essay. Reprinted in Gagaku Kai 53: 12-14, 1976.

93. _____. "Japanese National Anthem: Words and Music with English Translation." Musical Courier 48(10; 25): 6, 1904.

94. _____. "Music among the Japanese." All the Year Round 5: 149-52, May 1861.
Account of the musical perceptions of some seventy Japanese officers and attendants who accompanied the Japanese envoys to America in 1860.

95. _____. comp. Nanki Concert Hall. Tokyo: Japan Advertiser Press, 1924. 27p.
Miscellaneous writings concerning the music, lecture hall, and programs of the concert series sponsored by Marquis Tokugawa during the period 1918-23.

96. _____. "Some Japanese Melodies." Scribner's Monthly 14(1): 504-506, May 1877.
Note on three Japanese melodies with score.

97. _____. "Timbre and Unpitched Sound—Two Characteristics of Traditional Japanese Music." The East (Asia Edition) 11(3): 12-15, 1975.
Comparison of Japanese and Western attitudes toward music, focusing on two characteristic factors that distinguish the two.

98. ARAKI, James T. The Ballad-Drama of Medieval Japan. Berkeley & Los Angeles: Univ. of California press, 1964. xvi, 289p.
Historical survey of the kōwakamai, a medieval performing art, and a study of its repertoire and

librettos. Based on the author's doctoral
dissertation, The Kôwakamai: A Survey of Its
Development as a Medieval Performing Art and a Study
of Its Texts, submitted to the Univ. of
California, Berkeley, 1961. Pt. 1 describes the
history and tradition of the kôwakamai,
tracing artistic elements that may have contributed
to its formation. Pt. 2 describes the kôwaka
text.

99. ____. "Bunraku." In Kodansha Encyclopedia of Japan
1: 212-15. Ed. Gen Itasaka. Tokyo: Kodansha
International, 1983.
Concise treatment divided into the following sections: conventions of the theater; early history;
stages of development; and the final stage. Treatment of musical matters is for the non-specialist
and lacks detail.

100. ____. "Kôwaka: Ballad-Dramas of Japan's Heroic Age."
Journal of the American Oriental Society 82:
545-52, Oct.-Dec., 1962.
Introductory study dealing with 1) the history and
artistic essentials, and 2) the style of the
libretto of the kôwaka genre. Points out
similarities to the narrative techniques to be found
in Homer.

101. ____. "Medieval Artistic Elements in Japanese Folk
Theater." Modern Drama 9: 373-88, February 1967.
Deals with three Japanese performing arts that are
believed to have originated in the medieval era of
Japanese history, kôwaka, Kurokawa-nô, and
ennen.

102. ARIEL [pseud.]. "The Music of the Gods." The Japan
Magazine 4(11): 648-51, March 1914.
Brief introduction to kagura, Shintô ritual
music and dance.

103. ARIMA Daigorô. Japanische Musikgeschichte auf Grund
der Quellenkunde. Doctoral dissertation,
Universität Wien, 1933. xxii, 246p.
Japanese musical history using material from
historical sources.

104. ____. "Musical Education as Part of General Education."
In Music—East and West: Report on 1961 Tokyo

East-West Music Encounter Conference, p. 119-22.
Executive Committee for 1961 TEWME, 1961.
General remarks on the music education system of
Japan.

105. ____. Musik der Japaner. Tokyo: Kunitachi College of
Music, 1963. 10p.
Short attempt at explaining the Japanese tone-system
employing Western modal concepts.

106. ARNN, Barbara. "Shirabyôshi." In Kodansha Encyclopedia of Japan 7:145. Ed. by Gen Itasaka.
Tokyo: Kodansha International, 1983.
Brief description of the meaning of the term
shirabyôshi and the history of the song and
dance performance known by this name.

107. ARNOLD, Paul. Le Théâtre japonais: nô, kabuki,
shimpa, shingeki. Paris: L'Arche, 1957. 286p.
Discussion about the origins of Japanese performing
arts, followed by description of the nô and
kabuki theaters, with brief mention of the
modern theaters shinpa and shingeki. Little
treatment of the music itself.

108. ARRIVET, Arthur. "Atsumori, mis en français." Revue
Française du Japon 4: 470 98, 1895.
Translation of the third act of Ichi no tani
futaba gunki ("First Battle of Atsumori at Ichi no
Tani"), a popular ningyô-jôruri play.

109. ASAJI Nobori, trans. Kadensho: A Secret Book of Noh
Art. Osaka: Union Services Co., 1975. xxiii, 119p.
Translation of Zeami Motokiyo's Fûshi kaden,
with a brief preface and translator's notes.

110. ASHIHARA Eiryô. The Japanese Dance. Tokyo: Japan
Travel Bureau, 1964. 164p.
Includes a section on kabuki dance.

111. ASTON, William George. "The Death-Stone." Drama: Its
History, Literature and Influence on Civiliza-
tion 3: 239-48, 1903.
Translation of the nô play Sesshôseki
("Death-Stone") which is attributed to Hiyoshi
Yasukiyo.

112. ____. trans. Nihongi: Chronicles of Japan from the

20

Earliest Times to A.D. 697. Introduction to the
New Edition by Terence Barrow. Rutland, VT & Tokyo:
Tuttle, 1972. xxii, iv, 443p. [First Printing in
1896 by the Japan Society]
The first translation into any Western language of
the Nihongi or Nihonshoki. Its description
of early Japan contains numerous accounts of music,
dance, and musical instruments as well as various
rituals.

113. AUSTERLITZ, Robert. "Two Gilyak Song Texts." In To
Honor Roman Jakobson: Essays on the Occasion of His
Seventieth Birthday, p.99-113. The Hague: Mouton,
1967.
Linguistic and musical analysis of two Gilyak songs
collected in Japan from a Southeast Sakhalin dialect
speaking informant.


\* \* \* \* \* \* \* \* \* \*


114. BABA Tsunego. "The Dappled Reins: An Old Japanese
Drama." Oriental Review 2: 413-18, 1912.
Partial translation of Tanba Yosaku, a
jôruri play by Chikamatsu Monzaemon.

115. BENITEZ, J. M. 'Chormusik.' Part of article "Musik." In
Japan-Handbuch, col.1199-1202. Ed. by H.
Hammitzsch. Wiesbaden: Franz Steiner, 1981.
Outline of the history of choral music in Japan in
the post-Meiji era.

116. ____. "Christliche Musik." Sub-entry of 'Religiöse
Musik'; part of article "Musik." In Japan-
Handbuch, col.1280-84. Ed. by H. Hammitzsch.
Wiesbaden: Franz Steiner, 1981.
Survey of Christian religious music in post-Meiji
Japan.

117. BENL, Oscar. Das künstlerische Ideal Seami's.
Doctoral dissertation, Univ. Hamburg, 1974. 121p.
Survey of Zeami's treatises and examination of his
concepts monomane, hana and yûgen. An annotated translation of Zeami's writings Kyûi
shidai and Kadensho is provided.

118. BERGER, Donald Paul. "Ethnomusicological Implications in
     Music Education." In International Conference
     Report of ISME, p.309-12. Tokyo: ISME, 1963.
     Brief discussion of the music of the Japanese
     nô drama, with reference to its importance to
     the Western musician in music education.

119. _____. Folk Songs of Japanese Children. Rutland, VT
     & Tokyo: Tuttle, 1969. 63p.
     Collection of 15 warabeuta arranged for chorus
     with piano accompaniment. The original song-texts,
     in both Japanese syllabary and Roman letters, and
     English translations are provided.

120. _____. 'Shakuhachi.' [Part 3 of §IV. Instruments and
     Their Music]. Sub-entry of the article "Japan."
     In New Grove Dictionary of Music and Musicians
     9: 532-34. Ed. by Stanley Sadie. London: Macmillan,
     1980.
     Short survey of the history, genres, notation,
     construction, and playing method of the shaku-
     hachi.

121. _____. "The Nohkan: Its Construction and Music."
     Ethnomusicology 9(3): 221-39, 1965.
     Introduction to the flute used in the nô
     theater and a transcription of a few pieces into
     staff notation.

122. _____. "The Shakuhachi and the Kinko Ryû Notation."
     Asian Music 1(2) : 32-72, 1969.
     Introduction to the shakuhachi, its construc-
     tion, notation, fingering, and method of playing.
     Basically instructional. Includes a transnotation of
     Ômi-Hakkei, a Yamada style sôkyoku piece
     composed by Yamato Manwa.

123. BETHE, Monica and Karen BRAZELL. Dance in the Nô
     Theater 3 vols. Ithaca: China-Japan Program,
     Cornell Univ. 1982. Vol.1 Dance Analysis xvi,
     193p.; Vol.2. Plays and Scores xiii, 276p.; Vol.
     3 Dance Patterns xv, 242p. [Cornell Univ. East
     Asian Papers No. 29].
     Extremely detailed treatment of dance as an element
     in the performance of nô, with careful consider-
     ation of its relationship to other elements,
     including music. In addition to separate treatment
     of all dance patterns, a number of dances are

22

illustrated in their contexts within a number of
plays (including Kiyotsune, Hagoromo, Tadanori,
Atsumori, Yamamba, Adachi-gahara, Sakuragawa, Utô,
Eguchi and Kamo). A series of five video
cassettes (total length approx. 4 hrs) have been
made that illustrate dances treated in the text.

124. _____. Nô as Performance: An Analysis of the Kuse
Scene of Yamamba. Ithaca, NY: China-Japan Program,
Cornell Univ., 1978. 200p. illus., notation.
[Cornell Univ. East Asian Papers, 16].
Detailed study of the kuse scene of Yamamba, with an
examination of this well-known nô play from
various aspects, such as text, music, dance, masks,
and costumes.

125. BEVAN, Paul. "Japanese Music." Transactions and Proceedings of the Japan Society, London 5(4): 312-
18, 1902.
Introductory essay about Japanese music, dealing
with the harmonization of Japanese melodies, and recent publications of the time, such as a Collect-
tion of Japanese Koto Music and Rekishi
Shôka.

126. BIRD, Isabella L. Unbeaten Tracks in Japan: An Account
of Travels in the Interior Including Visits to the
Aborigines on Yezo and the Shrine of Nikko.
Rutland, VT & Tokyo: Tuttle, 1973. 336p. Illus.
Travelogue of a seven-month trip to northern Japan
in 1878. Of particular interest is the mention of
Ainu people during the early Meiji period. Includes
a brief description of musical instruments.

127. BLASDEL, Christopher. "Anatomy of a Japanese Festival:
The Great Midwinter Wakamiya On-matsuri of Kasuga
Shrine." Hogaku 1(1): 113-19, Spring 1983.
Description of the structure of the midwinter
festival of Kasuga Shrine, Nara, and the role that
it plays at present in the transmission and preservation of the performing arts associated with it.

128. BLAU, Hagen. Sarugaku und Shushi: Beiträge zur Aus-
bildung dramatischer Elemente im weltichen und
religiösen Volkstheater der Heian-Zeit, unter
besonderer Berücksichtigung seiner sozialen Grund-
lagen. Wisebaden: Otto Harrassowitz, 1966. xi,
481p.

Study of folk/ceremonial performing arts (incl.
sarugaku) and artists (shushi/jushi
etc.) of ancient and medieval Japan, with a historical study of the development of dramatic elements
in those ritual and entertainment arts, focusing on
their social background. Based on the doctoral
dissertation Sarugaku und...Grundlagen,
submitted to Freie Univ. in 1961.

129. BOCK, Felicia G. "Elements in the Development of
Japanese Folk Song." Western Folklore 7(1): 356
-69, January 1948.
Discussion of min'yô ("folk song"), dealing
with its historical aspects, concepts, classifications, musical instruments, and song texts.

130. _____. Engi-shiki: Procedures of the Engi Era. 2
vols. Tokyo: Sophia Univ., 1970; 1972.
Volume 2 includes a translation of Senso Daijô-
sai ("The Great New Food Festival of the
Enthronement"), p.31-56, and of Norito ("The
Rituals"), p.65-105, both of which abound with
musical references.

131. _____. "Japanese Children's Songs." Western Folklore
8(4): 328-41, October 1949.
Introduces the dôyô or warabe-uta, children's game songs and nursery rhymes, quoting two
dozen song-texts and giving translations.

132. _____. "Songs of Japanese Workers." Western Folklore
8(3): 202-28, July 1949.
Survey of Japanese folk songs. Introduces song-texts
of several representative work songs such as
oiwake-bushi, taue-uta, kusatori-uta, chatsumi-
uta, etc. No music included.

133. BOCKLET, Heinrich V. Japanische Volksmusik: Gesänge
und Instrumentalstücke nach handschriftlichen Origi-
nalen. Wien: Albert J. Gulmann, 1888. 17p.
Collection of traditional Japanese tunes, harmonized
and arranged for the piano. Contains Miyasama,
Hitotsutoya, Rokudan and Midare.

134. BONNEAU, Georges. "Le Dodoitsu savant ou poeme de vingt-
six syllabes." Bulletin de la maison Franco-
Japonaise 5(1-2): 13-27, Tokyo, 1933.
Texts and French translations of 13 classical and 7

new dodoitsu poems.

135. _____. L'Expression poetique dans le folk-lore
Japonais. Vol.3: La Chanson du Kyushu. Paris:
Paul Geuthner, 1933. 189p.
Folk song texts of Kyûshû, with French trans-
lations.

136. _____. La Sensibilité japonaise. Tokyo: By the
author, 1934. xxxix, 395p. Revised from Bulletin
de la Maison Franco Japonaise 6(1 2): 1934.
Contains French translations of 20 dodoitsu song
texts.

137. BORRIS, Siegfried. "The Discovery of the Japanese
Musical Tradition by Artists and its Influence on
Musical Creation in Japan and in the West." In
Proceedings of the International Round Table
on the Relations Between Japanese and Western Arts,
Sept.1968, Tokyo & Kyoto, p.274-87. Tokyo:
Japanese National Commission for UNESCO, 1969.
Historical review of the musical encounter between
East and West occurring both in Japan and in the
West. Traces the history of Western interest in
Japanese music.

138. _____. Musikleben in Japan. Kassel: Bärenreiter,
1967. 246p. photos, indexes.
Fact-finding book about the music culture of Japan
in the 1960's, dealing with both traditional and
Western-style music. Gives basic information, sta-
tistics, a directory of musicians, music institutes,
broadcasting stations, concert halls, and other
music industries, including instrument-makers.
Somewhat dated.

139. _____."Geist und Geschichte der japanischen Musik."
Musik und Bildung 3(10): 476-82, 1971.
Includes brief historical sketch and treatment of a
number of individual genres. Some surprising
omissions and factual mistakes.

140. BOSE, Fritz. "Japanische Musik im 19. Jahrhundert." In
Musikkulturen Asiens, Africas und Ozeaniens im 19.
Jahrhundert, p.135-65. Ed. by Robert Günther.
Regensburg: Gustav Bosse, 1973.
Survey of various traditional music genres found in
19th century Japan, with a discussion of the changes

and new developments in their form and style caused
by the political and social upheaval associated with
the Meiji restoration. Western influences on
Japanese music culture prior to and after the reform
are treated.

141. BOWERS, Faubion. Japanese Theatre. New York:
Heritage House, 1952. Tokyo & Rutland, VT: Tuttle,
1974. 294p.
Historical introduction to Japanese theater. Con-
tains translations of three kabuki plays:
Tsuchigumo, Sesshû gappôgatsuji, and
Sukeroku.

142. ____. Theatre in the East: A Survey of Asian Dance
and Drama. Edinburgh & New York: Thomas Nelson and
Sons, 1956. New York: Goore Press, 1960. 374p.
Chapter 14, p.320-60, is devoted to Japanese
Theatre.

143. BOWNAS, Geoffrey and Anthony THWAITE, trans. The
Penguin Book of Japanese Verse. Hammondsworth:
Penguin Books, 1964. lxxvi, 243p.
Includes translations of kagura, azuma-asobi uta,
Ryôjin hishô, Heike monogatari, imayô, and
folk songs.

144. BOXER, C.R. The Christian Century in Japan, 1549-
1650 Berkeley: Univ. of California Press, 1951.
535p. NE

145. BRANDON, James R., ed. Chûshingura: Studies in
Kabuki and the Puppet Theatre. Honolulu: Univ.
Press of Hawaii, 1982. xii, 231p.
Contains four fine articles centering around the
best-known kabuki play; Donald Keene's
"Variation on a Theme: Chûshingura" (p.1-21),
Donald Shively's "Tokugawa Plays on Forbidden
Topics" (p.23-57), William Malm's "A Musical Ap-
proach to the Study of Japanese Jôruri" (p.59-110)
and James Brandon's "The Theft of Chûshingura:
or The Great Kabuki Caper" (p.111-51).

146. ____, ed. Kabuki: Five Classic Plays. Cambridge, MA:
Harvard Univ. Press, 1975. xii, 378p. photos.
Includes complete translations of Sukeroku,
Narukami, etc.

147. BRANDON, James. R., William P. MALM, and Donald SHIVELY.
     Studies in Kabuki: Its Acting, Music and
     Historical Context. Honolulu: Univ. Press of
     Hawaii, 1978. 183p. Illus., music, bibliography,
     discography.
     Three monographs about kabuki: Shively comments
     on its social background; Brandon on its acting
     styles; and Malm on its musical structure. Malm's
     discourse on music (p.133-75) consists of a brief
     history of kabuki music, a study of its function
     and succinct illustration of its form.

148. BRANNEN, Noah S. "Ancient Japanese Songs from the
     Kinkafu Collection (Together with an English
     Translation of the Kinkafu)." Monumenta
     Nipponica 23(3-4): 229-320, 1968.
     Detailed description of the Kinkafu, "Song-
     scores for the wagon, a long zither," and complete
     translation of the 9th-century collection of
     Japanese songs/poems.

149. BRANNEN, Noah and William ELLIOT. Festive Wine:
     Ancient Poems from the Kinkafu. New York & Tokyo:
     Weatherhill, 1969. 90p.
     Translation of the text of the Kinkafu, with an
     introduction, essay on primitive Japanese poetry,
     and commentaries on the translations. Also includes
     a number of woodblock prints based on the images of
     the poems by Haku Maki. Little treatment of musical
     matters; the musical notation of Kinkafu is not
     discussed.

150. BRAUNS, David. Traditions japonaises sur la chansons,
     la musique et la danse. Paris: J. Maisonneuve,
     1890. vii, 106p. NE

151. BRAZELL, Karen, trans. The Confessions of Lady
     Nijô. New York: Anchor Press, 1973; reprint ed.
     Stanford, CA: Stanford Univ. Press, 1976.
     Translation of the late 13th to early 14th-century
     autobiographical narrative Towazu-gatari.
     Includes a number of scenes illustrating the
     importance of music in the court life of the time.

152. BRESLER, Laurence. "Chôbuku Soga, A Noh Play by
     Miyamasu." Monumenta Nipponica 29: 69-81, 1974.
     Annotated translation of a nô play attributed
     to Miyamasu, a nô playwright thought to have

been born about one generation after Zeami.

153. BRINKLEY, Frank. Japan: Its History, Arts and
     Literature. Vol.3, Boston & Tokyo, 1901; Vol.6,
     1902.
     Vol.3 contains translations of the nô play
     Ataka and the kyôgen play Sannin
     Katawa. Vol.6 contains translations of bon
     dance songs and a flower dance song of Bingo
     Province.

154. BRITTON, D. Guyver. "The Sound of the Samisen."
     Eastern Horizon (Hong Kong) 6(10): 58-61,
     October 1967. NE

155. BROWN, R.L. "Musical Instruments of Japan." Music
     Teacher 56(5): 9-10, 1977.
     Short introduction to the musical instruments of
     Japan written by a music teacher after attending a
     conference of music teachers in Tokyo. The account
     is hence rather limited in scope. Includes drawings
     of 16 musical instruments.

156. BUCHANAN, Daniel C. "Inari: Its Origin, Development, and
     Nature." Transactions of the Asiatic Society of
     Japan 2nd S. 12: 1-191 [entire issue], 1935.
     Study on Inari daimyôjin, the god of harvests,
     and rituals associated with it. Includes description
     of the kagura ("deity music") rite performed at
     the Fushimi Inari Shrine.

157. BURDE, Wolfgang. "Balance zum Schweigen." Musik und
     Gesellschaft 33(8): 475-79, 1983.
     Discussion of the conflict of traditional Japanese
     music and Western music since the Meiji Restoration,
     concentrating on the problems faced by avant-garde
     composers.

158. BURNETT, Henry. "An Introduction to the History and
     Aesthetics of Japanese Jiuta-Tegotomono." Asian
     Music 11(2): 11-40, 1980.
     Analytical study of jiuta-tegotomono, a style of
     koto music which flourished in the late 18th and
     early 19th centuries.

159. ____. "The Evolution of Shamisen Tegotomono: A Study of
     the Development of Voice/Shamisen Relationships."
     Hogaku 1(1): 53-92, Spring 1983.

Study dealing with the evolution of the relationship
between the shamisen and voice in Edo period jiuta
tegotomono, covering the period c.1690 through
1822. Although based largely on secondary material,
it also includes examination of a number of musical
examples.


\* \* \* \* \* \* \* \* \* \*


160. CANZONERI, Vincent. "Background of Japanese Music."
Japan Times Weekly 1:28-30; 2:29-30, 39, 1938.
Magazine article introducing Japanese music culture
to Westerners.

161. _____. "Music of Japan: An Appreciation." Contemporary
Japan 9: 269-304, March 1940.
Insightful essay introducing some characteristics
of traditional Japanese music to Westerners.

162. _____. "A Theory of the Modes in Japan; Popular,
Traditional Music." Tôyô Ongaku Kenkyû
1(2): 1-8, 1938.
Study of the miyako-bushi mode. An approach for
grasping the characteristics of this mode in terms
of a "melodic system of related modes."

163. CARLES [pseud.?]. "Music for Japanese Hymns." The
Chrysanthemum 2: 440-43, 1882.
Essay dealing with the problems in composing
Christian hymns to be sung in the Japanese language.

164. CHAMBERLAIN, Basil H. trans. "The Death Stone: A Lyric
Drama from the Japanese." Cornhill Magazine
34: 479-88, 1876.
Translation of the nô play Sesshôseki.

165. _____. Japanese Things: Being Notes on Various
Subjects Connected with Japan. London: Kegan Paul,
Trench, Trubner & Co., 1927. xvi, 568p. [Reprint of
1905 5th Ed. Revised; 1st Ed. 1880].
Contains sections on music, p.339-44, and theater,
p.462-74. Gives information about traditional music
instruments, the nature of the Japanese scale, as
well as a list of recommended books on these

subjects.

166. CHO, Gene Jinsiong. Some Non-Chinese Elements in the
Ancient Japanese Music: An Analytical-Comparative
Study. Doctoral dissertation, Northwestern Univ.
1975. 236p.
Comparative study of "ancient" songs of China and
Japan defined in fairly broad terms. Analysis of
Japanese material is based exclusively on the modern
performance practice of kagura, saibara, rôei,
etc., as transcribed in Vol.1 of Shiba Sukehiro's
Gosenfu ni yoru gagaku sôfu ('Gagaku Scores in
Western Notation') of 1968.

167. CONDIT, Jonathan. "Differing Transcriptions  from the
Twelfth-Century Japanese Koto Manuscript Jinchi
Yôroku." Ethnomusicology 20(1): 87-95, 1976.
Attempt to decipher the koto notation of
Jinchi Yôroku strictly in accordance with the
instructions given at the beginning of the manu-
script, avoiding reference to modern performance
practice.

168. COURANT, Maurice. "Japon--Notice historique." In Encyclopédie de la musique et dictionnaire du conser-
vatoire. Pt.1, 1: 242-56. Ed. by Albert Lavignac.
Paris: Delagrave, 1921.
Brief description of several musical instruments
including the shô, hichiriki, koto, and
shamisen, with reference to register and
tunings. Written in 1912, most of the information
was based on the writings of Piggott and Müller (See
Entries 658 and 586).

169. CRAIG, Dale A. "The Sound of Japanese Music." Arts of
Asia 1(2): 13-16, March-April 1971.
Introductory survey of the major genres of Japanese
music and musical instruments.

170. CRIHFIELD, Liza. Ko-uta: "Little Songs" of the Geisha
World. Rutland, VT, & Tokyo: Tuttle, 1979. 100p.
Introduction to ko-uta with 25 songs in both
Roman letters and Japanese with translations.

171. CRUMP, J. and William P. MALM, eds. Chinese and
Japanese Music Dramas. Ann Arbor, MI: Center for
Chinese Studies, Univ. of Michigan, 1975 [Michigan
Papers in Chinese Studies, 19]. viii, 255p.

Collection of the five papers read at the
conference on the relations between Chinese and
Japanese music-drama held at Univ. of Michigan, Oct.
1-4, 1971. See Entries Malm(528), Sesar(715), and
Teele(778) for annotations.

172. CUNNINGHAM, Eloise. "The Japanese Ko-uta and
Ha-uta: The 'Little Songs' of the 17th Century."
Musical Quarterly 34: 68-83, 1948.
Stylistic description of one of the light vocal
genres accompanied by shamisen.

173. CURTIS, Natalie. "The Classic Dance of Japan." Musical
Quarterly 1: 329-35, 1915.
Brief introduction to the tradition of kenbu, a
martial dance to the accompaniment of shigin,
Chinese verse recited with Japanese pronunciation.


\* \* \* \* \* \* \* \* \* \*


174. DAN Ikuma. "The Influence of Japanese Traditional Music
on the Development of Western Music in Japan."
Transactions of the Asiatic Society of Japan,
3rd S. 8: 201-17, 1961. Transl. by Dorothy G.
Britton.
Discussion of the characteristics of traditional
music, with a general survey of Western-style
music by Japanese, the major "schools" of composers
and their ideas, followed by the author's view as to
what is "Japanese" in music.

175. DEAN, Britten. "Mr. Gi's Music Book: An Annotated
Translation of Gi Shimei's Gi-shi Gakufu."
Monumenta Nipponica 37(3): 317-32, Autumn 1982.
Translation of the foreword, introduction,
postscript, postface, and the text of three of a
total fifty songs given in the 18th-century Ming
music source Wei-shi Yuepu by Wei Ziming. Little
treatment of musical matters.

176. DeFRANCIS, John. Things Japanese in Hawaii.
Honolulu: Univ. Press of Hawaii, 1973. xiv, 210p.
illus., glossary, index.
Guide to Japanese cultural tradition in the Hawaiian

Islands. Illustrates the special cultural events,
including music, dance and drama festivals.

177. DEMIEVIILE, Paul, ed. "Bombai." In Hôbôgirin
(Dictionnaire encyclopédique du bouddhisme), 93-113.
Published under the supervision of Sylvain Lévi and
J. Takakusu. Tokyo: Maison Franco-Japonaise, 1929.
Elaborate description of Buddhist chant. Includes
the definition of bombai or shômyô,
Indian chant, history of the Buddhist chant in Chi-
na, the Buddhist chant in Japan, its history, theo-
ry, vocal technique, notation, and a bibliography.

178. _____. "La Musique come ou Japon." Etude Asiatiques
1: 199-226, 1925. Issued separately by G. von Oest,
Paris as vols. 19-20 of the Publications de
L'Ecole française d'Extrême Orient, 1925. NE

179. DEW, Louise E. "Musical Instruments of Japan" Music
17: 445-58; 1899-1900.
Introductory study of the instruments of Japan
which, despite the inclusion of a surprising amount
of interesting information, gives rather confused
accounts of the origin of the names of a number of
instruments.

180. DICKINS, Frederic Victor, trans. Chiushingura, or the
Loyal League: A Japanese Romance. Introduction by
Hoffman Atkins. Yokohama, 1875. 213p.
Translation of the story of Kanadehon Chûshin-
gura, a play by Takeda Izumo. The appendix con-
tains a metrical translation of parts of the play
Chûshingura, and translation of parts of the
nô play Takasago.

181. DITTRICH, R. "Beiträge zur Kenntnis der japanische
Musik." Mitteilungen der Deutschen Gesellschaft
für Natur- und Völkerkunde Ostasiens 6(58): 376-
91, January 1897.
Musical scales and modal character of popular songs
of the late Edo and early Meiji periods.

182. _____. Sechs Japanische Volkslieder. Leipzig:
Breitkopf & Härtel, 1894. 11p.
Collection of six folk songs arranged for the piano.
Contains German and English translations of the song
text of Jizuki-uta, Matsuri-bayashi, Sakura,
Gombei ga tane maku, Kon'in no uta, and Ryû-

kyû-bushi.

183. DIXON, James Main. "Aino Musical Instruments."
Chrysanthemum 2: [Illus. 20 & 22], 1882.
Illustrations, with notes following the index, are
of some historical value.

184. DRÄGER, Walter and Helmut ERLINGHAGEN, trans.
Kazuraki, Nôdrama von Kanze Seami Motokiyo."
Monumenta Nipponica 5: 151-79, 1942.
Annotated German translation of Zeami's
Kazuraki, with detailed presentation of the
historical and legendary background of the play.

185. DU BOIS, Francis. "The Gekkin Musical Scales." Transactions of Asiatic Society of Japan 19: 369 71,
1891.
Very brief description of the tunings, scales and
Sino-Japanese notation of the gekkin (yuè
qin) or "moon guitar."

186. DUNN, Charles J. The Early Japanese Puppet Drama.
London: Luzac, 1966. 153p.
Study of early ningyô-jôruri. Based on the
author's doctoral dissertation, The Development of
Zyooruri up to 1686, Univ. of London, 1959-60.
210p.

187. DUNN, Charles J. and TORIGOE Bunzo. The Actor's
Analects. New York: Columbia Univ. Press, 1969. x,
308p.
Annotated translation of Yakusha rongo, or more
accurately, Yakusha-banashi, a collection of
precepts left by great kabuki actors at the end
of the 17th century. With introduction, notes, and
the original text in Japanese.


* * * * * * * * * *


188. EBISAWA, Arimichi. "The Meeting of Cultures." In The
Southern Barbarians: The First Europeans in Japan,
p.124-44. Ed. by Michael Cooper. Tokyo & Palo Alto:
Kodansha International, 1971.
Argues that the first introduction of Western music

into Japan was possibly as early as 1552. Also sets
out historical evidence that Catholic missionaries
introduced not only vocal music, but also
instrumental music, which was appreciated by the
Japanese of the time.

189. ECKARDT, Hans. "Abendländische Musik in Japan." Musik
im Unterricht: Schulmusik Ausgabe 54: 347-51,
November 1963.
Outlines the introduction and development of Western
music in Japan.

190. _____. "Die Ei und Saezuri, verschollene melismatische
Gesangformen im Japanischen Tanz." In Kongress-
Bericht Lüneburg 1950. Gesellschaft für Musikforschung, p.170-72. Kassel & Basel: Bärenreiter,
1951.
Inquiry into the obsolete bugaku performance
practices, ei and saezuri, in which court
dancers sang verses while dancing.

191. _____. "Gagaku, die altklassische Musik Japans." Das
Musikleben 2: 333-35, 1949.
Short introduction to the history, instruments, and
music of gagaku.

192. _____. "Die Geistige Umwelt des Tachibara Narisue."
Gesellschaft für Natur- und Völkerkunde Ostasiens,
Nachschriften 74: 16-32, 1953.
Initial publication of two chapters from Pt.1 of the
author's dissertation Das Kokonchomonshû des
Tachibana Narisue als musikgeschichtliche Quelle
(See Entry 194).

193. _____. "Japanische Musik." In Die Musik in Geschichte
und Gegenwart 6: 1720-53. Kassel: Bärenreiter,
1957.
Fairly detailed survey of the history of Japanese
music. Based as it is, largely on secondary sources,
there are number of factual mistakes, and decided
bias towards treatment of the author's speciali-
ties. However, generally a fairly good entry.

194. _____. Das Kokonchomonshû des Tachibana Narisue als
musikgeschichtliche Quelle. Wiesbaden:
Harrassowitz, 1956. 432p.
Publication of the author's Habilitationsschrift.
Berlin Freie Univ., 1954. Treatment of Kokon-

34

chomonshū (correctly Kokonchomonjū) as a
source for the history of music. Pt.1 provides a
historical survey of Japanese music during the Heian
period, a reconstruction of the life of Tachibana, a
discussion of the most important sources for the
history of music from the 12th to 17th centuries and
a list of musical terms. Pt.2 contains an annotated
translation of the section Kangen kabu ('Music
and Dance') from the Kokonchomonjū, compiled
in 1254.

195. _____. "Konron: Reste kontinentaler Mythologie in der
japanischen Bugaku." Orients Extremus 7: 17-30,
1960.
Concise and wide-ranging discussion of the various
mythological elements associated with the komagaku dance piece Konron (or Konron hassen)

196. _____. "Koto." In Die Musik in Geschichte und Gegenwart 7: 1946-50, 1958.
Account of the various instruments known by the name
koto, and the historical development of the
musics associated with them. Treatment is highly
prejudiced towards the wagon of kagura and
sō no koto of gagaku; Edo period sōkyoku is given only a cursory mention.

197. _____. "Das Nō: Vom lyrischen Chordrama der Japaner."
Musica 6(1): 12-16, January 1952.
Concise introduction to the nō play.

198. _____. "Ryōwō." Sinologica 3(2): 110-28, 1952.
Inquiry into the title, origin, meaning and practice
of Ryōwō (or Raryōwō, Ranryōwō),
a commonly performed court dance piece. Reference to
its mask and relation to the dragon cult in India
and China is included.

199. _____. "Shamisen." In Die Musik in Geschichte und
Gegenwart 12: 620-24. Kassel: Bärenreiter, 1966.
Introduction to the shamisen, outlining its introduction to Japan, its physical construction and
tunings.

200. _____. "Tanabe, Hisao." In Die Musik in Geschichte und
Gegenwart 13: 78-79. Kassel: Bärenreiter, 1966.
Brief biographical notes on the founder of modern
Japanese musicology.

201. _____. "Wesenszuge der japanische Musik." Nachrichten-
kunde Ostasiens 43: 20–22. 1937 [Tokyo, 1938].
Summary on a paper read on April 14, 1937 in Tokyo
on the characteristics of Japanese music, which also
included performance of a number of gagaku
pieces by the Chûô Gagaku Kyôkai.

202. _____. "Zum Verständnis der japanischen Musik."
Yamato: 104–11, Berlin, 1929.
Short introduction to Japanese music, dealing with
gagaku, nagauta, gidayû and nô.

203. _____. "Zur Frage der Ei und Saezuri." Monumenta
Nipponica 4: 600 605, 1941.
Inquiry into the obsolete performance practices
ei and saezuri, in which court dancers sang
verses while dancing. Reference is also made to the
religious verse of Okina, a ceremonial nô
play. The same article also appears in Tôa
ongaku ronsô [Festschrift Tanabe Hisao], p.97–
104. Tokyo: Yamaichi Shobô, 1943.

204. _____. "Zur Frage der Netori." Monumenta Nipponica
1: 269–72, January 1938.
Defines netori and deals with Heian period
references to its aesthetic power, citing two
anecdotes from Kokonchomonjû, written by
Tachibana Narisue in 1253.

205. _____. "Zur Frage und Bedeutung der Ranjô." In Festschrift Heinrich Besseler zum sechzigsten Geburts-
tag, p.35–42. Edited by Institute für Musikwissenschaft der Karl-Marx-Univ. Leipzig: Deutscher Verlag
für Musik, 1961.
Inquiry into the meaning of ranjô, entrance
and exit music used in bugaku (court dance), and
its possible connection to purification rituals.

206. ECKERT, Franz. "Japanische Lieder." Mitteilungen der
Deutschen Gesellschaft für Natur- und Völkerkunde
Ostasiens 2(20): 423–38, 1879.
Transcription of two Japanese songs, Ikabakari
and Harusame ni, with German translation of the
song texts.

207. _____. "Die japanische Nationalhymne." Mitteilungen
der Deutschen Gesellschaft für Natur- und Völkerkunde Ostasiens 3(23): 131, March 1881.

36

Music of <u>Kimigayo</u>, the national anthem of Japan, and translation of the song-text. Possibly the earliest Occidental edition.

208. EDWARDS, Osman. "Japanese Theatres." <u>Transaction</u> <u>and</u> <u>Proceedings</u> <u>of</u> <u>the</u> <u>Japan</u> <u>Society,</u> <u>London</u> 5: 142-64, 1902.
Account of traditional Japanese theatres, centering on the popularity of no and kabuki plays, and Kikugorô and Danjûrô, <u>kabuki</u> actors.

209. ELLIS, Alexander J. "On the Musical Scales of Various Nations." <u>Journal</u> <u>of</u> <u>the</u> <u>Society</u> <u>of</u> <u>Arts</u> 33: 485-527, March 1885.
Section 15 "Japan" gives interval measurements based on the cent system for the <u>biwa</u> (based on an instrument in an exhibition of 1884), <u>koto</u> and <u>shamisen</u> (based on a group of performers not, apparently, of the highest standard), making reference also to Isawa's report of 1884 (See Entry 368). Concludes that despite the presence of considerable differences according to player, the Japanese system of intervals is essentially a chromatic one.

210. EMBREE, John F. <u>Japanese</u> <u>Peasant</u> <u>Songs.</u>
Philadelphia: American Folklore Society, 1944. ix, 96p. bibliog., photos. [Memoirs of the American Folklore Society, Vol.38, 1943]; reprint ed., New York: Kraus, 1969.
Collection and translation of folk songs from Kuma county, Kumamoto Prefecture. Gives an intensive analysis of the song-texts and cultural contexts, but no music is included.

211. EMMERT, Richard. "Hiranori: A Unique Rhythm Form in Japanese Nô Music." In <u>Musical</u> <u>Voices</u> <u>of</u> <u>Asia</u> [Report of Asian Traditional Performing Arts 1978], p.100-107. Tokyo: Japan Foundation, 1980.
Study of the <u>hiranori</u> rhythms employed in nô drama music as a unique rhythmic form described by the author as "a metered text-centered rhythm." Includes examples from the famous play <u>Hagoromo</u>.

212. _____. "The Japanese <u>Shakuhachi</u> and Some Comparisons with Several Vertical Flutes of Southeast Asia." In <u>Asian</u> <u>Musics</u> <u>in</u> <u>an</u> <u>Asian</u> <u>Perspective</u> [Report of Asian Traditional Performing Arts 1978], p.115-24.

Tokyo: Japan Foundation, 1977.
Study of the shakuhachi, dealing with the
history, playing techniques and construction of the
instrument, with a brief comparison to other
vertical flutes of Southeast Asia.

213. ____. "The Maigoto of Nô - A Musical Analysis of the
Chû no Mai." Yearbook for Traditional Music
15: 5-13, 1983.
Introduction to the musical structure of the maigoto, or instrumental dance music, of nô,
which gives graphical representations of parts
played by the instruments of the hayashi ensemble in the chû-no-mai ('middle' or 'medium'
tempo dance).

214. EMMERT, Richard and MINEGISHI Yuki, eds. Musical
Voices of Asia [Report of Asian Traditional
Performing Arts 1978]. Supervised by KOIZUMI Fumio,
TOKUMARU Yoshihiko and YAMAGUCHI Osamu. Tokyo: Japan
Foundation, 1980. xx, 407p., illus., photos,
bibliog., discog., glossary.
Report of the second event in the ATPA project
sponsored by the Japan Foundation, held in Tokyo in
1978. Includes several articles and reports concerning traditional Japanese music and description of
musical instruments.

215. ENDRESS, Gerhild. "Die Kehi-Lieder des Koyô-shû
von 1099." Oriens Extremus 23(1): 39-64, June
1976. plates.
Study of the texts of the kehi no kagura (sacred
songs of the Kehi Shrine, ancient head shrine of
Echizen, situated in Tsuruga, Fukui Prefecture) as
preserved in the late 11th century source
Jôtoku-bon koyô shû (now held in Yômei
Bunko, Kyoto). Includes translation into German.

216. EPPSTEIN, Ury. "Japanese Music through the Eyes of Meiji
Era Musicians." In Transactions of the Interna-
tional Conference of Orientalists in Japan 6: 90-
93. Tokyo: Tôhô Gakkai, 1961.
Introduction of two previously overlooked manu-
scripts in English written in the Meiji period: "On
Japanese Popular Music" by Uehara Rokushirô, and
"A General Sketch of the Gagaku" by Ue Shinkô
[Sanemichi].

38

217. _____. "Japanese Music through Meiji Eyes." Orient/
West 12(2): 14-29, 1967.
Introduction and discussion of two English manuscripts on Japanese music written by prominent Meiji
period musicians. Expansion of an article written
previously (Entry 216).

218. _____. "Responsorial Chant in Japanese Religious Rites,"
In Studies on Japanese Culture 2: 8-10. Tokyo:
Japan P.E.N. Club, 1973.
Briefly discusses the performance practice of kagura (mi-kagura), the holiest of the Shinto
imperial court rites, with a brief mention of the
prayer services of Ananai Kyô, one of the newer
religions.

219. ERNST, Earle. The Kabuki Theatre. Honolulu: Univ. of
Hawaii Press, 1974. xxii, 296p., photos. [Reprint of
the original 1956 ed. published by Oxford Univ.
Press]
One of the standard English-language references on
kabuki. Outlines the kabuki theater as a
whole, dealing with the physical theater, the audience and its attitudes, the hanamichi, elements of the performance, the stage, the actor,
plays and characters. Glossary of theater terms and
selected bibliography of works in Western languages
are included in the appendix. Discussion of the
music itself is limited.

220. _____. Three Japanese Plays from the Traditional
Theatre. London: Oxford Univ. Press, 1959. xv,
199p. Reprint by Greenwood Press, 1976.
Contains English translations of three kabuki
plays: Momijigari, Shiranami gonin-otoko, and
Sugawara denju tenarai kagami by Earle Ernst
and others.

221. ERNST, Earle and YOSHIKOSHI Tatsuo. "Nô." In
Kodansha Encyclopedia of Japan 6: 23-29. Tokyo:
Kodansha International, 1983.
Concise treatment of nô, divided into the
following sections: origins, evolution, stage, performers, properties, costumes, masks, plays, per-
mance, and audience; with synopses of some well-
known plays. Emphasis is on theatrical aspects, with
little treatment of music.

* * * * * * * * * *


222. FELTZ, William E. Kyômono: A Traditional Japanese
     Music. M.A. Thesis, Univ. of Hawaii, 1970. viii,
     321p.
     Stylistic description and analysis of two kyô-
     mono compositions, Shin-Ukifune and Sasa no
     tsuyu.

223. FLORA, Reis. "The Acoustic Behavior of the P'iri and the
     Hichiriki." Selected Reports in Ethnomusicology
     2(1): 141-58. Los Angeles: Institute of Ethno
     musicology, UCLA, 1974.
     Examination of the acoustic behavior of two double-
     reed aerophones: the hyang p'iri of Korea and
     the hichiriki of Japan. Spectral analysis
     undertaken using the Seeger Melograph Model C.

224. FLORENZ, Karl A. "Ancient Japanese Rituals." Trans-
     actions of the Asiatic Society of Japan 27(1):
     1-112, 1900.
     Translation with detailed notes of the norito,
     Minazuki tsumogori no ô-harai ("Great Puri-
     fication of the Last Day of the Sixth Month"), the
     tenth norito in Engi-shiki (Collection of
     the Engi Rituals) compiled by Fujiwara no Tokihira
     in the early 10th century.

225. FOARD, James H. "Seiganji: The Buddhist Orientation of a
     Noh Play." Monumenta Nipponica 35: 439-56, 1980.
     Includes a translation of Seiganji, a nô
     play attributed to Zeami.

226. FÖDERMAYR, Franz. "Shichi-no-San: Die Obertontief-
     stimme in Japan?" In Festschrift Othmar Wessely
     zum 60. Geburtstag, p.151-205. Tutzing: Verlegt
     bei Hans Schneider, 1982.
     Attempt at demonstrating the existence of a type of
     biphonic vocal production in Japanese Buddhist chant
     by spectral sound analysis using a Spektrogramm.
     Sound material is the original tape version (made by
     Eta Harich-Schneider) and later record version
     (included in discs attached to her A History of
     Japanese Music [See Entry 293]) of the Shichi-
     no-San sung by Nakayama Dôyô at the Zen temple
     Eiheiji in 1953.

40

227. FOLJANTY, D. 'Instrumentenbau.' Part of article 'Musik.'
In Japan-Handbuch, col. 1225-28. Ed. by H.
Hammitzsch. Wiesbaden: Franz Steiner, 1981.
Outline of the history of the construction of
Western instruments in Japan in the modern era.

228. _____. 'Konzertleben.' Part of article "Musik." In
Japan-Handbuch, col.1234-39. Ed. by H.
Hammitzsch. Wiesbaden: Franz Steiner, 1981.
Survey of the development of concert life in Japan
of the modern era, concentrating almost exclusively
on Western music.

229. _____. 'Militärmusik.' Part of article "Musik." In
Japan-Handbuch, col.1239-41. Ed. by H.
Hammitzsch. Wiesbaden: Franz Steiner, 1981.
Short treatment of the history of military music in
Japan's modern era.

230. _____. 'Musik und Massenmedien.' Part of article
"Musik." In Japan-Handbuch, col.1241-43. Ed. by
H. Hammitzsch. Wiesbaden: Franz Steiner, 1981.
Survey of music in the modern mass media, dealing
with broadcasting, recording, and film music.

231. _____. 'Musiker/Ensembles.' Part of article "Musik." In
Japan-Handbuch, col.1243-45. Ed. by H.
Hammitzsch. Wiesbaden: Franz Steiner, 1981.
Short survey dealing with musicians and musical
ensembles (symphony orchestras etc.) performing
Western music in post-Restoration Japan.

232. _____. 'Musikkritik.' Part of article "Musik." In
Japan-Handbuch, col.1246-47. Ed. by H.
Hammitzsch. Wiesbaden: Franz Steiner, 1981.
Survey of music criticism in Japan, concentrating on
its beginnings at the turn of the twentieth century.

233. _____. 'Musikpublizistik.' Part of article "Musik." In
Japan-Handbuch, col.1247-48. Ed. by H.
Hammitzsch. Wiesbaden: Franz Steiner, 1981.
Survey of music publishing in modern Japan.

234. _____. 'Musikschulen und -Hochschulen, Konservatorien.'
Part of article "Musik." In Japan-Handbuch, col.
1249-50. Ed. by H. Hammitzsch. Wiesbaden: Franz
Steiner, 1981.
Brief survey of music education in modern Japan,

centering on educational institutions.

235. _____. 'Oper/Operette.' Part of article "Musik." In
Japan-Handbuch, col.1271-73. Ed. by H.
Hammitzsch. Wiesbaden: Franz Steiner, 1981.
Outline of the introduction and development of opera
in post-Restoration Japan.

236. FREEBERN, Charles L. The Music of India, China, Japan
and Oceania: A Source Book for Teachers. A.Mus.D.
dissertation, Univ. of Arizona, 1969. 176p.
Source book for teachers including materials on the
musical cultures of Oceania, China, Japan and India,
with sections on history, geography, notational
systems, instruments, performance practice and
suggested listening material. Includes a limited
annotated bibliography.

237. FRITSCH, Ingrid. "A Comparison of Tozanryu and Kinkoryu
Shakuhachi Arrangements for Sankyoku Gasso Made from
Identical Originals." Yearbook for Traditional
Music 15: 14-30, 1983.
Study of the role played by the shakuhachi in
sankyoku performance, comparing versions of the
same pieces in two differing schools of shakuhachi. It should be noted that the mistaken
printing of p.21 and 22 in reverse order has made
this section of the article difficult to follow.

238. _____. Die Solo-Honkyoku der Tozan-Schule: Musik für
Shakuhachi zwischen Tradition und Moderne Japans.
Kassel: Bärenreiter, 1979. 241p. [Studien zur
traditionellen Musik Japans, 4]
General remarks on the shakuhachi, its history,
acoustics, and its styles and repertoire; followed
by detailed description of the Tozan school, its
organization and honkyoku repertoire. The focal
point of this monograph is a detailed analysis of
six honkyoku compositions, which demonstrate the
fundamental changes that have taken place in
shakuhachi music. Text in German, accompanied by
English and Japanese summaries.

239. FUJIE, Linda. "Effects of Urbanization on Matsuri-bayashi
in Tokyo." Yearbook for Traditional Music 15:
38-44, 1983.
Ethnomusicological study of matsuri-bayashi
(Shinto festival music) as it occurs in modern

42

Tokyo, in view of the processes of survival and
adaptation brought about by urbanization.

240. FUJII Seishin. "A buddhismus és a zene (Buddhism and
Music)." In Emlékkönyv Kodály Zoltán hatvanadik
születésnapjára, p.139-42. Ed. by Béla Gunda.
Budapest: Magyar Néprajizi Tarsaság, 1943.
Contribution to the Festschrift Zoltán Kodály on the
occasion of his 60th birthday. NE

241. FUKUSHIMA Kazuo. "Japanese Music Notation." In Sound
on Paper: Music Notation in Japan, p.9-29. New
York: Japan Society, 1981.
Catalogue of an exhibition shown at the Japan House
Gallery in the summer of 1981. Consists of two
sections: Pt.1 "Contemporary Music" contains
bibliographical notes on 51 pieces; Pt.2
"Traditional Music" contains 24 items of old
notation from the collection of the Research
Archives for Japanese Music, Ueno Gakuen College,
Tokyo.

242. _____. "Nô-Theater und japanische Musik." In
Darmstädter Beiträge zur Neuen Musik 4: 103-11.
Mainz: B. Schott's Sohne, 1961.
Lecture given in the Ferienkurse für Neue Musik,
August 29 through September 10, 1961. General
remarks on nô, touching upon its history,
performance, classification of the repertory, form,
music and philosophy. Also appears in Musik im
Unterricht 11: 351-56, November 1963.

243. FURUYA Benzô, trans. A Japanese Drama, Taikoki
judanme. Yokohama [1897]. ii, 12p.
Translation of the tenth and last part of the ningyô jôruri play Ehon Taikô-ki by Chikamatsu Yanagi.

* * * * * * * * * * *

244. GARFIAS, Robert. The Basic Melody of the Tôgaku
Compositions of the Gagaku Repertoire. Master's
thesis, UCLA, 1958. Vol.1, 253p. Vol.2, music.
General description of the history, theory and

performance practice of tôgaku, followed by
discussion of the underlying basic melody that can
be abstracted by analysis of the shô, koto
and biwa parts of tôgaku pieces. Analysis
treats 3 pieces from each of the 6 tôgaku
modes. Vol.2 contains transcriptions of the koto
and biwa parts of all of these pieces.

245. _____. "Gagaku." In Kodansha Encyclopedia of Japan
3: 1-2. Tokyo: Kodansha International, 1983.
Descriptive account of gagaku, divided into the
following subsections: Repertoire, history,
bugaku, instruments, theory and formal structure. The bibliography given at the conclusion
appears to delete a substantial body of work written
in English on the topic in the last decade.

246. _____. 'Gagaku.' Part of §III. Theatrical and Courtly
Genres. Sub-entry of "Japan." In New Grove
Dictionary of Music and Musicians 9. 510-15. Ed.
by Stanley Sadie. London: Macmillan, 1980.
Outline of gagaku, divided into the following
sections: historical introduction, theory, instruments, form, aesthetics and style.

247. _____. Gagaku: The Music and Dance of the Japanese
Imperial Household. Foreword by Lincoln Kirstein.
New York: Theatre Arts Books, 1959. xi, 30p.
bibliog., discog., plates.
Booklet prepared on the occasion of the Imperial
Household Gagaku Ensemble's first visit to the
U.S.A. A brief introduction to the various aspects
of gagaku and bugaku as well as explanatory
notes on representative pieces of the repertoire.

248. _____. "Gagaku: Subdivisions of the Repertoire." In
Festival of Oriental Music and the Related Arts,
p.24-32. Los Angeles: Univ. of California Press,
1960.
Describes traditional classification principles of
major genres, styles and sub-styles of the court
music and dance of ancient Japan.

249. _____. "Gradual Modifications of the Gagaku Traditions."
Ethnomusicology 4(1): 16-19, 1960.
Introduction to the gagaku musicians and dancers
of the Japanese Imperial Household, and discussion
of the gradual changes of their performing style.

44

250. _____. "Koto Ornamentation Technique in 11th Century
Japanese Gagaku." In Studia Instrumentorum Musicae 3 [Festschrift Ernst Emsheimer on the Occasion
of his 70th Birthday], p.44-50. Stockholm: Musik-
historika Museet, 1974.
The 12th century gagaku koto manuscript Jinchi
yôroku is described as an important source with
regard to certain elements of performance practice
of the time. Includes transcriptions of two pieces.
Reprinted in Gagaku Kai 52: 1-21, 1975.

251. _____. Music of a Thousand Autumns: The Togaku Style
of Japanese Court Music. Berkeley: Univ. of
California Press, 1975. x, 322p., bibliog., discog.,
music, plates, index.
Expansion of the author's doctoral dissertation,
The Togaku Style of Japanese Court Music: An
Analysis of Theory in Practice, UCLA, 1965. 500p.
A historical survey and analytical approach to the
contemporary tôgaku style of gagaku is
used to elucidate the characteristics of today's
ensemble practice.

252. _____. "The Sacred Mi-Kagura of the Japanese Imperial
Court." Selected Reports 1(2): 149-78. Los
Angeles: Institute of Ethnomusicology, 1968.
Description of the sacred mi-kagura ceremony as
it is annually practiced today at the Imperial
Court. Accompanied by a transcription of three
typical pieces with a translation of the song-texts.
Reprinted in Gagaku Kai 49: 1-18, 1969 (Pt.1);
50: 1-19, 1972 (Pt.2).

253. _____. "Some Effects on Changing Social Values on
Japanese Music." In Music - East and West: Report
on 1961 Tokyo East-West Music Encounter Conference, p.18-22. Tokyo: Executive Committee for
1961 Tokyo East-West Music Conference, 1961.
Garfias's cautionary advice on Western vs. Non-
Western cultural conflict: "Some of the most
important and meaningful elements of the tradition
are being replaced by more easily accessible ones"
and "too often the new tradition is being built
upon the superficial aspects of both East and West."

254. GARNER, Edwin C. Mode: Three Modes of Shingi Shingon
Shomyo as Analyzed by ECG. Doctoral dissertation,
Wesleyan Univ., 1976. 340p.

Rather peculiar treatment of the modes of Buddhist
chants of the Shingi Shingon sect. Neither historical sources of the chants nor the modes are direct-
ly discussed.

255. GIESEN, Walter. "Buddhistische Musik." Sub-entry of
'Religiöse Musik'; part of article "Musik." In
Japan-Handbuch, col.1277-80. Ed. by H.
Hammitzsch. Wiesbaden: Franz Steiner, 1981.
Brief survey of music associated with Buddhism,
dealing centrally with shōmyō but also in-
cluding reference to other genres strongly influ-
enced by Buddhist philosophy.

256. _____. "Japanische Musik heute: Weltsprache oder Sonder-
dialekt? In Japanische Kultur in der Gegenwart,
p.9-51. Vienna: Sensen, 1982.
Study of musical composition in modern Japan, which
gives a historical overview of the relationship
between Western and Japanese elements in the music,
and deals with a number of important works from the
period 1969-80. Mentions more than 20 composers;
appends German-language bibliography, as well as
discography for all works mentioned.

257. _____. Zur Geschichte des buddhistischen Ritualgesangs
in Japan: Traktate des 9. bis 14. Jahrhunderts zum
Shōmyō der Tendai Sekte. Kassel: Bärenreiter,
1977. xii, 355p., music, bibliog., index. [Studien
zur traditionellen Musik Japans, 1]
Detailed study of Tendai shōmyō, Buddhist
chant of the Tendai sect, with an annotated trans-
lation of six early shōmyō texts of the
Ōhara school: 1) Annen's Shittanzō (880); 2)
Tanchi's Shōmyō yōjinshū (1233); 3)
Shūkai's Gyosan-mokuroku (1238); 4) Anonym.
Ōhara-shōmyō hakasezu (before 1299); 5)
Chikū's Shōmyō-inritsu (1349); and 6)
Gyōnen's Shōmyō-genruki (c.1300).

258. GIL-MARCHEX, Henri. "Japon (Musique du)." In Larousse
de la musique 1: 480-82. Paris: Larousse, 1957.
A somewhat dated short historical survey of Japanese
music from the 8th century through early 20th
century. Includes a number of inaccuracies, as well
as inconsistent spelling of Japanese words.

259. _____. "Music in Japan." Contemporary Japan 6: 264-

46

76, September 1937.
A French pianist-composer examines the characteristics of Japanese music, briefly describing
bugaku, nô, bunraku, kabuki, shakuhachi, and
modern trends.

260. _____. "La Musique au Japon." La Revue musicale 120:
305-20. November 1931.
Impressionistic view of Japanese music, with comparisons to French music, and emphasis on similarities
between the French and Japanese cultures.

261. _____. "A Propos de la musique japonaise." Revue
Pleyel 44: 244-48, May 1927.
Essay concerning various aspects of Japanese music,
touching upon nô, kabuki, gagaku, and musical
instruments.

262. GINSBURG, Semjon. "Die Musik in japanischen Theater."
Melos 8(10): 437-40, October 1929.
Short descriptive treatment of the music of kabuki.

263. GOFF, Janet Emily. "The Tale of Genji as a Source of the
Nô: Yûgao and Hajitomi." Harvard Journal of
Asiatic Studies 42(1): 177-229, June 1982.
Detailed study of the relationship of the nô
plays Yûgao and Hajitomi to the Tale of
Genji and later commentaries on it. Appends annota-
ted translations of the two plays.

264. GOLAY, Jacqueline. "Pathos and Farce: Zatô Plays of
the Kyôgen Repertoire." Monumenta Nipponica
28(2): 139-49, 1973.
Discussion of the kyôgen plots centered around
blind monks (often musicians), which occupy a large
place in the repertoire.

265. GRAF, Walter. "Zur gesanglichen Stimmgebung der Ainu."
In Festschrift Walter Wiora, p.529-35. Ed. by
Ludwig Finscher and Christoph-Hellmut Mahling.
Kassel: Bärenreiter, 1967.
Examination, with the aid of a sonagram, of the
characteristic voice production of the Ainu.

266. GRAMATZKY, August. "Lied der Daishichi Kotogakko
Zoshikwan." T'oung pao, 2nd S. 3: 30-31, 1902.
Translation of Shichikô Zôshikan no uta
("The School Songs of Zôshikan"). Original text is

given in both Japanese and Roman letters.

267. GRIM, John and Mary Evelyn GRIM. "Viewing the Hana
Matsuri at Shimoawashio, Aichi Prefecture." Asian
Folklore Studies 41(2): 163-85, 1982.
Description of a festival centered around a 24-hour
kagura performance, held in Shimoawashiro, northern
Aichi Prefecture, on January 2-3, 1982. Treats the
setting of the performance and the major features of
the dance. Titles of dance pieces are given, but
there is little treatment of the music itself.

268. GULIK, Robert H. van. "The Chinese Lute in Japan." In
The Lore of the Chinese Lute, p.197-224. Tokyo:
Sophia Univ., 1940.
Study on the Chinese ku-ch'in (qin) with a brief
history of the instrument in Japan attached as an
appendix.

269. GUNJI Masakatsu. Buyo: The Classical Dance. Trans.
by Don Kenny. Introduction by James R. Brandon. New
York & Tokyo: Walker/Weatherhill, 1970. 207p.,
illus.
Survey of classical Japanese dance, with particular
reference to kabuki dance, including its
aesthetics, history and current condition. Contains
numerous photographs, both color and monochrome.

270. _____ Kabuki Trans. by John Bester, Introduction
by Donald Keene. Tokyo: Kodansha, 1969. 265p.
Includes many photographs by Yoshida Chiaki.

271. GUNJI Sumi, TAKANO Noriko, and YAMADA Yoshiko.
"Descriptions of Musical Instruments: ATPA 1978."
In Musical Voices of Asia [Report of ATPA 1978],
p.203-85. Tokyo: Japan Foundation, 1980.
Includes descriptions of a few Japanese instruments
such as chijin, dura, kotsuzumi, nôkan, ô-
tsuzumi, and shimedaiko.

272. GÜNTHER, Robert. 'Gagaku-Musik.' Part of article
"Musik." In Japan-Handbuch, col.1202-8. Ed. by
H. Hammitzsch. Wiesbaden: Franz Steiner, 1981.
Survey of the history, instruments, and performance
practice of gagaku.

273. _____. "Historische Abriss." Sub-entry of 'Historischer
Überblick'; part of article "Musik." In Japan-

48

Handbuch, col.1185-95. Ed. by H. Hammitzsch.
Wiesbaden: Franz Steiner, 1981.
Concise historical outline of Japanese music from
the earliest period to the twentieth century.

274. _____. "Shintôistische Musik." Sub-entry of 'Religiöse
Musik'; In Japan-Handbuch, col.1273-77. Ed. by
H Hammitzsch Wiesbaden· Franz Steiner 1981
Survey of the various genres of music associated
with Shintô, including a brief outline of impor
tant historical sources.

275. GUTZWILLER, Andreas B. Shakuhachi: Aspects of History,
Practice and Teaching. Doctoral dissertation,
Wesleyan Univ. 1974. 197p.
An outline history of shakuhachi, description of
gaikyoku pieces and honkyoku compositions,
with the author's evaluation of the teaching and
learning process in Japan.

276. _____. "Stone Age and Promised Land: An Answer to James
Reid." Ethnomusicology 23(1): 103-7, 1979.
Critical comments on Reid's article, "Transcription
in a New Mode." See Entry 673.

* * * * * * * * * *

277. HAAGS GEMEENTEMUSEUM. Japanese prenten met muziek
[Japanese Woodcuts with Music]. The Hague: Haags
Gemeentemuseum (Muziekafdeling), 1975. 60p., illus.
25 plates of Japanese woodcuts with musical instru-
ments, part of the collection of Japanese prints in
the Music Department of the Gemeentemuseum at The
Hague, with descriptive notes in both Dutch and
English.

278. _____. Traditionele muziekinstrumenten van Japan
[Traditional Musical Instruments of Japan]. The
Hague: Haags Gemeentemuseum (Muziekafdeling), 1979.
64p., illus., disc.
Illustrations of 30 Japanese musical instruments
from the collection of the Haags Gemeentemuseum with
descriptive notes by Onno Mensink in both Dutch and
English.

279. HAAS, Hans. "Hichikiochi: Ein No-Spiel." Die Wahrheit 5: 32-35, 1904.
Translation of the nô play Shichiki-ochi.

280. HAGUENAUER, M.C. "La Dance rituelle dans la cérémonie du
chinkonsai." Journal Asiatique 216: 299-350,
April-June 1930.
Discussion of shamanism in ancient Japan and the
ritual mitama shizume or chinkonsai. A
special reference is made to the Ame no uzume
dance described in the Kojiki and Nihonshoki.

281. HALFORD, Aubrey S. and Giovanna M. HALFORD. The Kabuki
Handbook. Foreword by Faubion Bowers. Tokyo:
Tuttle, 1956. 510p., illus., bibliog.
A playgoer's guide, with synopses of the most
commonly performed kabuki plays with explanatory
notes, arranged in alphabetical order.

282. HALL, Fernau. "Gagaku and Bugaku." Sangeet Natak 19:
13-23, January March 1971.
Short article on the history and practice of
Japanese court music and dance, alluding to
historical linkages to India, written after the
author had attended a concert given by the Imperial
court dancers and musicians in London in 1970.

283. HAMMITZSCH, H. 'Instrumente.' Part of article "Musik."
In Japan-Handbuch, col.1209-25. Ed. by H.
Hammitzsch. Wiesbaden: Franz Steiner, 1981.
Illustrated survey of Japanese musical instruments
divided into three classes: wind, string, and per-
cussion.

284. _____. ed. "Musik." In Japan-Handbuch, col.1183-
1294. Wiesbaden: Franz Steiner, 1983.
Brief historical survey (E. Harich-Schneider) and a
historical outline (R. Günther) are followed by the
following encyclopedic entries: "Bunraku-Musik" (E.
Harich-Schneider), "Chormusik" (J. M. Benitez),
"Gagaku-Musik" (R. Günther), "Instrumente" (H.
Hammitzsch), "Instrumentenbau" (D. Foljanty),
"Kabuki-Musik" (W. P. Malm), "Konzertleben" (D.
Foljanty), "Militärmusik" (D. Foljanty), "Musik und
Massenmedien" (D. Foljanty), "Musiker/Ensembles,"
"Musikkritik," "Musikpublizistik," "Musikschulen und
-Hochschulen, Konservatorien" (D. Foljanty), "Musik-

50

wissenschaft" (K. Hattori), "Musiziergattungen und
-Stile" (E. Harich-Schneider), "Nô-Musik" (E.
Harich-Schneider), "Oper/Operette," "Religiöse
Musik" (R. Günther, W. Giesen and J. M. Benitez),
and "Volksmusik" (Y. Tokumaru).

285. HARICH-SCHNEIDER, Eta. "Ein Beitrag zur Quellenkunde
japanischer Musik." In Bericht über den siebenten
internationalen Musikwissenschaftlichen Kongress,
Köln, 1958, p.123-26. Kassel: Bärenreiter, 1959.
Introduction to source materials for research in
Japanese music. Discussion of the problems of
original texts and editions, and the nature of
handwritten copies.

286. _____. 'Bunraku-Musik.' Part of article "Musik." In
Japan-Handbuch, col.1195-99. Ed. by H.
Hammitzsch. Wiesbaden: Franz Steiner, 1981.
Short description of various aspects of bunraku
and its music, including historical development,
vocal technique, instruments, melodic material,
formal elements, and musical notation.

287. _____. "Chant bouddhique japonais: le shô-myô." In
Encyclopédie des musiques sacrées 1: Le Sacré en
Extrême-Orient, Méditerranée, Afrique et
Amérique, p.199-213. Ed. by Jacques Porte. Paris:
Labergerie, 1968.
Brief introduction to the shômyô tradition.

288. _____. "Le Chant du Tenrikyô." In Encyclopédie de
musiques sacrées 1: Le Sacré en Extrême-Orient,
Méditerranée, Afrique et Amérique, p.291-95. Ed.
by Jacques Porte. Paris: Labergerie, 1968.
Brief introduction to the ritual songs of Tenrikyô, a religious sect founded in 1838 by a woman
named Nakayama Miki.

289. _____. "Dances and Songs of the Japanese Shintô Cult."
World of Music 25(1): 16-29, 1983.
Account of some dances and songs of the ancient
Shintô cult, including translation of texts from
Azuma asobi, and two examples from the Kinka-
fu.

290. _____. "The Earliest Sources of Chinese Music and Their
Survival in Japan." Monumenta Nipponica 11(2):
195-213, 1955.

Note on the description of music-making and musical
instruments found in Shi Jing ("Book of Odes")
with a hypothesis that certain features of the Chou
music have been preserved and can be found in
present day Japanese gagaku.

291. ____. "Die frühesten erhaltenen Quellen der Kagura-
Lieder." Deutsches Jahrbuch der Musikwissenschaft 10: 113-26, 1965.
Study of the Kagura wagon hifu ("Secret Wagon
Notation of Kagura"), a 10-century source of
kagura which has been preserved at the Yômei
Bunko, Kyoto. Contains kagura texts with German
translation. An English version appears in p.284-91
of Entry 293.

292. ____. "Die Gagaku in der Musikabteilung des japanischen
Kaiserhofes." In Kongressbericht Gesellschaft für
Musikforschung, Lüneburg, 1950, p.168-70. Ed. by
H. Albrecht, H. Osthoff, and W. Wiora. Kassel &
Basel: Bärenreiter, 1951.
Brief discussion of the major stylistic divisions of
the gagaku repertoire including utamai,
tôgaku, komagaku, saibara, and rôei.

293. ____. A History of Japanese Music. London: Oxford
Univ. Press, 1973. 720p. music, bibliog., plates,
indexes. Accompanied by three 7-inch discs.
Extensive historical survey which, reflecting the
author's specialties, is balanced heavily in favor
of ancient and medieval Japanese music traditions.
Rather inadequate treatment of music of the Edo
period.

294. ____. "Japanese Music." In Encyclopaedia Britannica
14th ed. 12: 956-58. Chicago: Encyclopaedia
Britannica, 1965.
Short introductory description of Japanese music,
giving a broad historical outline. Somewhat dated
and lacks detail.

295. ____. "Japonaise (Musique)." In Encyclopédie de la
musique 2: 601-14. Paris: Fasquelle, 1959.
Fairly elaborate encyclopedia article giving a historical survey, stylistic description, lists of
sources, transcriptions, a bibliography and discography.

296. _____. "Koromogae: One of the Saibara of Ancient
Japanese Court Music." Monumenta Nipponica 8:
398-406, January 1952.
An introductory history of the vocal genre
saibara, centering on a description of the piece
Koromogae and its performance practice. Includes
both the original notation and a transcription into
Western staff notation.

297. _____. "The Last Remnants of a Mendicant Musicians'
Guild: The Goze in Northern Honshu (Japan)."
Journal of the International Folk Music Council
11: 56-59, 1959.
Brief description of the goze of Takada and
Nagaoka in Niigata Prefecture, and of their
repertoire.

298. _____. "Das Mikagura Hompu von 1332." In Asien,
Tradition und Fortschritt: Festschrift für Horst
Hammitzsch, p.173-83. Wiesbaden: Otto
Harrassowitz, 1971.
Attempt at transcription of the now obsolete piece
Hisago from vocal notation included in a mi-
kagura source presently held in the Ayanokôji
Collection of Tenri Library, which includes a colo-
phon dated 1332. Includes translation of the text.

299. _____. 'Musiziergattungen und -Stile.' Part of the
article "Musik." In Japan-Handbuch, col.1257-63.
Wiesbaden: Franz Steiner, 1981.
Encyclopedia entry dealing with a miscellany of
Japanese musical genres, eikyoku, saibara, azuma-
asobi, rôei, fuzoku, shamisen, koto, and
shakuhachi. Treatment especially of the last
three is rather perfunctory.

300. _____. 'Nô-Musik.' Part of the article "Musik." In
Japan-Handbuch, col.1263-70. Wiesbaden: Franz
Steiner, 1981.
Outline of the sources, history, musical notation,
formal construction, tonal material, and vocal
technique of nô, which suffers from some oversimplification.

301. _____. "The Present Condition of Japanese Court Music."
Musical Quarterly 39(1): 49-74, January 1953.
General survey of the gagaku and bugaku
tradition.

302. _____. "Regional Folk Songs and Itinerant Minstrels in Japan." _Journal of the American Musicological Society_ 10: 132-33, 1957.
Summary of a paper read on January 12, 1957 at the meeting of the Greater New York Chapter of AMS.

303. _____. _The Relations of Foreign and Native Elements in the Development of Japanese Music: A Case Study._ M.A. thesis, New School for Social Research, New York, 1954. NE

304. _____. "The Remolding of Gagaku under the Meiji Restoration." _Transactions of the Asiatic Society of Japan_, 3rd S.5: 84-105, December 1957.
Paper read at a meeting of the society on January 25, 1954. A critical review of the revisions and reforms of _gagaku_ made by the Imperial Household authorities during the early years of the Meiji era.

305. _____. "Renaissance Europe Through Japanese Eyes: Record of a Strange Triumphal Journey." _Early Music_ 1(1): 19-25, 1973.
Description of the travels and musical activities of four young Japanese who were taken to Europe to visit the Pope in 1584-85.

306. _____. _The Rhythmical Patterns in Gagaku and Bugaku_ Leiden: E. J. Brill, 1954. 109p., illus., plates. [Ethnomusicologica 3]
Introduction to and translation of the currently-used Meiji period partbooks for the percussion instruments of the _gagaku_ ensemble.

307. _____. _Rôei: The Medieval Court Songs of Japan._ Tokyo: Sophia Univ. Press, 1965. 132p. [Monumenta Nipponica Monograph 21]
Introduction to _rôei_, a vocal genre of court music, with a survey of its sources and texts.

308. _____. "Saibara." _Deutsches Jahrbuch der Musikwissenschaft_ 7: 63-73, 1963.
Introduction to _saibara_, a vocal form of court music created during the Heian period, with an analysis of its formal structure.

309. _____. "Le shômyô bouddhique, exercice de meditation." _Oriens extremus_ 9: 220-31, 1962.
An introductory study of Tendai _shômyô_ as

sung by Nakayama Gen'yû, the head of the shômyô tradition at the Hiei-zan Temple of Kyoto.

310. _____. "A Survey of the Remains of Japanese Court
Music." Ethnos 16(3-4): 105-24, 1951.
Survey of the present gagaku tradition. Deals
with the major groups of court musicians, the
repertoire based on the revised scores of 1876,
musical instruments, dance, vocal styles, and modal
aspects. Includes transcriptions of a small number
of pieces.

311. _____. "Tradition in Japanese Court Music, Gagaku."
Gagaku Kai 51: 7-15, 1973.
Paper read at Palais Palffy, Figaro Saal, Vienna, on
June 5, 1970, as an introduction to a concert by the
Imperial Musicians.

312. _____. "Über das Alter von Saibara-Melodien." In
Festschrift für Marius Schneider. Regensburg:
Bosse, 1971. NE

313. _____. "Über die Gilden blinden Musiker in Japan." In
Bericht über den internationalen musikwissenschaftlichen Kongress, Hamburg 1956, p.107-9. Ed.
by W. Gerstenberg, H. Husmann, and H. Heckmann.
Kassel: Bärenreiter, 1957.
Brief report concerning the goze, blind female
mendicant musicians of Niigata Prefecture,
describing their repertoire, which consists of three
types: danmono, kudoki, and kouta.

314. HARRISON, Frank. Time, Place and Music: An Anthology
of Ethnomusicological Observation c.1550 to c.
1800. Amsterdam: Frits Knuf, 1973. 221p., illus.
Contains short excerpts from Engelbert Kaempfer's
The History of Japan (1727), which describes a
type of street musician no longer seen in Japan.

315. HATTORI Kôzô. 'Musikwissenschaft.' Part of article
"Musik." In Japan-Handbuch, col.1251-57.
Wiesbaden: Franz Steiner, 1981.
Discussion of musicology in Japan after the Meiji
Restoration from the point of view of a Japanese
scholar of Western musicology.

316. HATTORI Ryûtarô. compil. Japanese Folk Songs, with
Piano Accompaniment. Tokyo: Japan Times, 1974.

168p. [1st ed. appeared in 1950]
Collection of 63 folk songs of Japan with piano
accompaniment, arranged by Miyahara Teiji and
Shinohara Masao. Song-texts translated into English
by Matsuhara Iwao, with brief explanatory notes.

317. _____. One Hundred Japanese Folk-Songs [Nippon no
min'yô] Tokyo: Ongaku no Tomo Sha, 1960. 251p.
Paperback collection of Japanese folksongs. Song-
texts romanized and translated into English by
Matsuhara Iwao.

318. _____. Traditional Folk Songs of Japan. Tokyo:
Ongaku no Tomo Sha, 1966. 233p.
Japanese folk songs with piano accompaniment.

319. HAUCHECORNE, Armand. "La Musique japonaise." In
Histoire de la musique 1: 305-18. Edited by
Roland-Manuel. Paris: Gallimard, 1960.
Brief general description of Japanese music, its
traditions, instruments, scales and various genres.

320. HAUCHECORNE, Jean Pierre. "Notes et impressions sur la
musique japonaise." Cultural Nippon 3(3):428-56,
October 1935.
Short but penetrating observation of various
aspects of Japanese music.

321. HAVENS, Thomas R. II. Artist and Patron in Postwar
Japan: Dance, Music, Theater, and the Visual Arts,
1955-1980. Princeton, NJ: Princeton Univ. Press,
1982. 324p.
Detailed study of the relationship between Japan's
modern community of professional dancers, musicians,
production companies, and visual artists, and their
patrons. Based largely on interviews undertaken by
the author during 1980-81. Sections on music treat
both traditional Japanese music and music in Western
style, classical and contemporary.

322. HAYASHI Kenzô. "Restoration of an Eighth Century
Panpipe in the Shôsôin Repository, Nara, Japan."
Asian Music 6(1-2): 15-27 [Perspectives on Asian
Music: Essays in Honor of Dr. Laurence E.R. Picken]
Report of an investigation concluding that the
panpipes of the Shôsôin originally had 18 pipes.

323. _____. "Study of Explication of Ancient Musical Score

of P'i-p'a Discovered at Tun-huang, China."
Nara Gakugei Daigaku Kiyô 5(1): 1-22, 1955.
Attempt at deciphering the notation of the
Tun-huang p'i-p'a-pu, a lute score discovered in
1905 by Pelliot and held in the Pelliot Collection
of the Bibliothèque National, Paris. Includes a
hand-written copy of the text of the source and
transcription into Western staff notation.

324. HAYASHI Kenzô, KISHIBE Shigeo, TAKI Ryôichi and
SHIBA Sukehiro. "Musical Instruments in the
Shôsôin." In Shôsôin no gakki, p.i-xxiv.
Edited by Shôsôin Office. Tokyo: Nihon Keizai
Shimbun Sha, 1967.
An English summary of the commentary and descriptive
notes on the plates in this lavishly illustrated
book, which describes the musical instruments housed
in the Imperial Treasure Repository, a collection of
objects used by the Emperor Shômu (r.724-49).

325. HAYASHIYA Tatsusaburô. "Ancient History and Performing
Arts." Acta Asiatica 33: 1-14, 1977.
Study of various aspects of the indigeous songs and
dances of ancient Japan combining both historical
and folkloristic approaches.

326. HEARN, Lafcadio. "After the War." In Kokoro: Hints and
Echoes of Japanese Inner Life, p.87-108. Rutland,
VT & Tokyo: Tuttle, 1972 [Reprint of the 1st ed.
published in Boston, 1896 by Houghton, Mifflin & Co]
Essay written in May and June 1895, immediately
after the Sino-Japanese War. Includes an English
translation of the military ballad Rappa no
hibiki (or Shirakami Genjirô, the name of a
Japanese bugler) and the tunes of bugle calls.

327. _____. Gleanings in Buddha-Fields: Studies of Hand and
Soul in the Far East. Rutland,VT & Tokyo: Tuttle,
1971. 269p. [Reprint of the 1st ed. published in
Boston, 1922]
Chapter II "Out of the Street" introduces the texts
of Japanese popular songs (hayari-uta), and
contains two dozen translations (p.29-42). Chapter
VIII "Buddhist Allusions in Japanese Folk-Song"
includes translations of several hauta and
dodoitsu texts.

328. _____. "Old Japanese Songs." In Shadowings, p.156-

92. Rutland, VT & Tokyo: Tuttle, 1971. [Reprint of
1st ed. published 1900 by Little, Brown & Co.,
Boston]
Collection of 22 old folk song-texts and their
translations. No music.

329. ____. "Songs of Japanese Children." In A Japanese
Miscellany, p.135-222. Rutland, VT & Tokyo:
Tuttle, 1954 [Reprint of 1st ed. published in
London, 1905]
Collection of 94 children's game-songs (warabe-
uta), nonsense-verses, and lullabies. The texts
are romanized and English translations attached.
Music is not provided.

330. ____. "Three Popular Ballads." In Kokoro: Hints and
Echoes of Japanese Inner Life, p.327-88. Rutland,
VT & Tokyo: Tuttle, 1972. [Reprint of 1st ed.
published 1896 by Houghton, Mifflin & Co., Boston &
New York]
Paper read before the Asiatic Society of Japan, Oct.
17, 1894. First appeared in Transactions of the
Asiatic Society of Japan 22: 285-336, 1894.
Introduction of the Daikoku-mai tradition of
Matsue, Shimane Prefecture and synopses of three
dance songs: Shuntoku-maru, Oguri-Hangan and
Yaoya Oshichi

331. HEIFETZ, Robin J. Post-World War II Japanese Composition. D.M.A. dissertation, Univ. of Illinois at
Urbana-Champaign, 1978. 98p.
Study of the range of stylistic possibilities
explored by post-war Japanese composers, including a
chapter on the influence of Cage and the New York
School.

332. HEINEMANN, Rudolf. "Zwischen Gagaku und Beethoven."
Musica 27(4): 377-80, July-August 1973.
Comments on the domination of the Western classics
in the modern Japanese music scene. Describes the
lack of audience for both the avant-garde and
traditional music of Japan.

333. HELM, Everett, comp. "Final Report of Musicultura, Three
Orient-Occident Encounters Organized by the Eduard
van Beinum Foundation." World of Music 20 (2):
7-154, 1978.
The section of Musicultura I (1974) contains

summaries of lectures on Japanese music by F. Vos,
William Malm, and Willem Adriaansz.

334. HELMES, Siegmund. "Stilmerkmale japanischer Musik."
Musik und Bildung 7: 14-18, 1975.
Study on the place of Japanese music in the
educational system of West Germany. Includes sugges-
tions for treatment of Japanese music style with
selected listening examples.

335. HIGA Etsuko O. Okinawan Classical Music: Analysis of
Vocal Performance. M.A. Thesis, Univ. of Hawaii,
1976. 305p.
Study of contemporary Okinawan vocal performance,
which is believed to have been derived from the
court tradition of the Ryukyu Kingdom (1429-1879).
Based on transcription and detailed analysis of
Tsikuten bushi and Hai-tsikuten bushi.

336. HILL, Jackson. "Ritual Music in Japanese Esoteric Buddhism: Shingon Shômyô." Ethnomusicology 26
(1): 27-36, 1982.
Introductory study of shômyô, concentrating
on that of the Shingon Sect Chizan School. Attempts
towards generalization result in some oversimplification.

337. HINCKS, Marcelle A. The Japanese Dance. London:
Heinemann, 1910. 32p. NE

338. HIRANO Kenji. "Urban Music in Japan in the Late
Seventeenth Century: An Approach from Musical
Philology." In Preservation and Development of the
Traditional Performing Arts [Report of ISCRCP
1980] p.229-32. Tokyo: Tokyo National Research
Institute of Cultural Properties, 1981.
Examination of instrumental pieces recorded in
17th-century musical notation.

339. _____. "The Intake and Transformation of Chinese Music
in Japan." In Proceedings of the Second Asian
Pacific Music Conference [Taipei 1976], p.26-28.
Seoul: Cultural and Social Centre for the Asian and
Pacific Region, 1977.
Concise outline of the transmission of Chinese music
to Japan which distinguishes three periods involving
varying degrees of "introduction," "digestion" and
"assimilation."

340. HIRONAGA Shuzaburo. <u>Bunraku</u>. Osaka: Bunrakuza
     Theater, 1959. Foreword by D. Warren-Knott, 120p.
     glossary, index.
     Handbook for playgoers including a brief history and
     synopses of representative plays.

341. _____. The <u>Bunraku Handbook</u>. Tokyo:
     Maison des Arts, 1976. 423p., index.
     Introductory remarks and a short history of Japanese
     puppet theater, with synopses of 102 classical
     plays.

342. HIROOKA Yoshio. "Music Education in Japan." <u>Music
     Educators</u> <u>Journal</u> 36: 34-35, November-December
     1949.
     Brief description of new music education in Japan
     under the occupation forces.

343. HIROSE Chiyo. "The Blind Koto Player of Japan." <u>Japan
     in Pictures</u> 4(10): 350-51, 1936.
     Brief biographical account of MIYAGI Michio (1894-
     1956) with photographs.

344. HOFF, Frank. "City and Country: Song and the Performing
     Arts in Sixteenth-Century Japan." In <u>Warlords,
     Artists, and Commoners</u>, p.133-62. Edited by George
     Elison and Bardwell L. Smith. Honolulu: Univ. of
     Hawaii Press, 1981.
     Discusses aspects of medieval <u>kouta</u> ("short
     songs") and <u>tauta</u> ("rice transplanting songs")
     within the schema of city and countryside.

345. _____. "Dance to Song in Japan." <u>Dance Research
     Journal</u> 9(1): 1-15, 1976-77.
     Defines a special mode of perception of Japanese
     dance, that is, hearing song and seeing the movement
     that it accompanies together as a unity.

346. _____. "Folk Performing Arts." In <u>Kodansha Encyclope-
     dia of Japan</u> 2:296-98. Tokyo: Kodansha
     International, 1983.
     Description of the various folk performance types
     known under the designation <u>minzoku-geinô</u>.
     Includes an outline of the system of categorization
     used most popularly today, that designed by Honda
     Yasuji.

347. _____. trans. The <u>Genial Seed: A Japanese Song</u>

Cycle. New York: Mushinsha-Grossman, 1971. 182p.
Translation of the <u>Tauezôshi</u>, a medieval
song cycle used to accompany the annual rice-
transplanting festival. Accompanied by an
introductory essay by Manabe Masahiro entitled "A
Note concerning the Text."

348. _____. "Kagura." In Kodansha Encyclopedia of Japan
4: 106-108. Tokyo: Kodansha International, 1983.
Concise survey of the major types of <u>kagura</u>,
giving special treatment of categories of <u>sato-
kagura</u>.

349. _____. <u>Like a Boat in a Storm: A Century of Song in
Japan</u>. Hiroshima: Bunka Hyô ron, 1982. 212p.
Translation of the <u>Kanginshû</u>, a collection of
medieval <u>kouta</u> ("short song"), and of the
<u>Odori</u> ("dance"), an anthology of thirty-one
songs from the repertory of women's <u>kabuki</u>.
Accompanied by the translator's essay "Kanginshu,
Odori and the Song Tradition," and two other introductory essays by Ōoka Makoto and Manabe Masahiro.
The translations and the discussion of the song
tradition are a revised version of an earlier publication. See Entry 350.

350. _____. <u>Song, Dance, Storytelling: Aspects of the
Performing Arts in Japan</u>. Ithaca: Cornell Univ.
China-Japan Program, 1978, 223p. [Cornell Univ. East
Asia Papers 15]
Introductions to and translations of two medieval
song collections, <u>Kanginshû</u> (short love songs)
and <u>Odori</u> (songs accompanying women's <u>kabuki</u>
dance), with an essay on <u>kagura</u>, "Shinto and the
Performing Arts."

351. _____. <u>A Theater of Metaphor: A Study of the Japanese
Noh Form</u>. Doctoral dissertation, Harvard Univ.
1966. iii, 123p.
Study of four plays of the <u>Yamabushi kagura</u>
theater.

352. _____. "Zeami on Jo-ha-kyû Theory: A Japanese Approach
to the Question of the Audience Experience." In
<u>Preservation and Development of the Traditional
Performing Arts</u> [Report of ISCRCP 1980], p.217-28.
Tokyo: Tokyo National Research Institute of Cultural
Properties, 1981.

Zeami's concept of jo-ha-kyû is examined as a
guiding principle for the aesthetics of the
performing arts of Japan.

353. HOFF, Frank and Willi FLINDT. "The Life Structure of
Noh: An English Version of Yokomichi Mario's
Analysis of the Structure of Noh." Concerned
Theatre Japan 2(3-4): 209-56, 1973.
Adaptation for English readers of the introductions
to Yôkyoku shû, written by Yokomichi (two
volumes in the Iwanami series of classical Japanese
literature). Lucid, persuasive explanation of the
dramatic and musical structure of nô.

354. HOFFMAN, Theodore. "Western Influences in the Japanese
Art Song." Monumenta Nipponica 22: 162-76, 1967.
Study of the musical style of pieces included in the
Nihon meika hyakkyoku shû ("One Hundred Art
Songs," Tokyo, 1947), pointing out a range in styles
from the simple imitation of Western techniques to a
more consistent use of these techniques in original
ways.

355. HOLTZ, V. "Japanische Lieder." Mitteilungen der
Deutschen Gesellschaft für Natur- und Völkerkunde
Ostasiens 1(4): 45-47, 1873.
Transcription and translation of three Japanese
songs. Continuation of the entry below.

356. _____. "Zwei japanische Lieder." Mitteilungen der
Deutschen Gesellschaft fur Natur- und Völkerkunde
Ostasiens 1(3): 13-14, 1873.
Transcription of two popular songs: Haru no uta
(today better known as Kazoe-uta) and Kimi to
wakarete, with German translations and commentary.

357. HONDA Masujiro. "The Annual Festival of Kamo Shrine: A
Repository of Theocratic Rites and Medieval Cus-
toms." Asian Review(5): 501-8, January-August
1921.
Description of Aoi-matsuri ("Hollyhock Festival") of Kyoto.

358. HOPP FERENC KELET-ÁZSIAI MŰVÉSZETI MÚZEUM, ed. Régi
japán hangszerek - A Bendel-Enking gyüjtemény
bemutatása [Old Musical Instruments of Japan--The
Exhibition of the Bendel-Enking Collection].
Commentary by Alice Egyed. Budapest: A Központi

Muzeum Igazgatóság. 1981. 23p. illus.
Catalogue of the Bendel-Enking collection. Includes
notes on traditional Japanese music, centering on
musical instruments.

359. HORI Ichiro. Folk Religion in Japan: Continuity and
Change. Edited by Joseph M. Kitagawa and Alan L.
Miller. Chicago: Univ. of Chicago Press, 1968. xvi,
270p.
Book primarily devoted to aspects of primitive
magical beliefs and practices found in various
Japanese religions, touching upon some music and
dance elements.

360. HORIGUCHI Yasuo. "Literature and Performing Arts in the
Medieval Age--Kan'ami's Dramaturgy." Acta
Asiatica 33: 15-31, 1977.
Examination of the nō play Eguchi in terms
of its association with the performing arts of medieval courtesans, pointing out that the extinction of
this tradition has resulted in a difference of
interpretation and appreciation of the play.

361. HORIUCHI Keizo. "A Snapshot of Japanese Music." Contemporary Japan 11(9): 1327-39, September 1942.
Phases of music in Japan from 1900-40. The major
genres of traditional Japanese music and various
aspects of Western music activity in Japan are
introduced.

362. HOVHANESS, Alan. "Gagaku Preludes and Polyphony."
Gagaku Kai 51: 1-45, 1973.
Introduction of gagaku for the Western reader
with transcriptions of the six netori, kogaku-
ranjō and banshikichō chōshi.

363. HUGHES, David W. "Japanese Folk Song Preservation
Societies: Their History and Nature." In Preser-
vation and Development of the Traditional Performing
Arts [Report of ISCRCP 1980], p.29-45. Tokyo:
Tokyo National Research Institute of Cultural
Properties, 1981.
Discussion on the nature and function of min'yō
hozon kai ("folk song preservation societies") and
the current condition of Japanese folk song.

364. HUGHES, Gwladys F. "Rhymes Sung by Japanese Children."
Western Folklore 10(1): 34-54, January 1951.

Song-texts of 35 warabe-uta from Tokyo and
Kyushu with translations.


\* \* \* \* \* \* \* \* \* \* \* \*


365. INOUE Jukichi, trans. Chushingura: or the Treasury of
Loyal Retainers of Akao, by Takeda Izumo, Miyoshi
Shoraku and Namiki Senryu. Tokyo, 1894, xxxvi,
81p.
Translation from Kanadehon Chûshingura
("Forty-seven Model Ronin"), a play popular in
ningyô-jôruri (bunraku) and kabuki
genres.

366. INOURA Yoshinobu and KAWATAKE Toshio. The Traditional
Theater of Japan. New York and Tokyo: Weatherhill,
1981. x, 259pp. illus.
Comprehensive history of the traditional Japanese
theatrical arts. Part I focusses on nô and
kyôgen, dealing with various related
dance-drama forms such as kagura, gigaku, bugaku,
ennen-nô, sarugaku-nô, dengaku-nô, and
chugen-nô. Part II discusses bunraku and
kabuki intensively. Originally published in 1971
in two separate volumes: A History of Japanese
Theater I: Noh and Kyogen, and A History of
Japanese Theater II: Bunraku and Kabuki.

367. ISAKU, Patia R. Mountain Storm, Pine Breeze: Folk Song
in Japan. Tucson: Univ. of Arizona Press, 1981. x,
126p. bibliography, index.
An American aficionada describes certain aspects of
Japanese folk songs. Includes many transcriptions
and translations of folk song examples. Largely
based on the author's doctoral dissertation An
Introduction to Japanese Folk Song (Wesleyan
Univ., 1973. 265p.)

368. ISAWA Shuji. Extracts from the Report of S. Isawa,
Director the Institute of Music, on the Result of
the Investigations Concerning Music, Undertaken by
Order of the Department of Education. Tokyo:
Institute of Music, [1884]. 77p.
Document of historical importance exhibited in

64

London in 1884 at a world exposition. Chapter titles
as follows: History of the Instruments; Researches
on Oriental and European music; Japanese musical
scales; Similarity between ancient Greek and the
present Japanese music--Hymn to Apollo (arranged for
gagaku ensemble); School music. Adds three
appendixes: Outlines of the History of Japanese
music; Improvement of Popular music; Specimens of
Japanese koto music.

369. ISHII Maki. "Japan's 'Music of Encounter'--Historical
Background and Present Role." World of Music 25
(1): 80-89, 1983.
Remarks on new developments in the patterns of
musical creation in Japan since the '60's, which the
author views, in his capacity as an active composer
of the present day, as 'music of encounter.'

370. ITASAKA Gen, editor-in-chief. Kodansha Encyclopedia of
Japan 9 vols. Tokyo: Kodansha International, 1983.
Includes a large number of entries associated with
dance, theater, and music, which are listed under
the general terms "dance," "folk song," "music," and
"theater" in the Index (Vol.9). Useful as an
introduction for the non-specialist, but should be
used with care because of its rather unbalanced
selection of entries and authors.

371. ITŌ Mikiharu. "Festivals." In Kodansha Encyclopedia
of Japan 2: 252-62. Tokyo: Kodansha International,
1983.
General outline and survey of Japanese festivals,
divided into two sections, the first of which deals
with matsuri (festival proper) and the second of
which deals with nenchū gyōji (annual
events). Tables include the most important of both
types and give concise descriptions of individual
festivals.

372. ITŌ Setsuko. "The Muse in Competition: Uta-awase
Through the Ages." Monumenta Nipponica 37(2):
201-22, 1982.
Study of uta-awase (verse-writing imperial court
banquets) that appends translation of extracts from
the "Records of Uta-awase," in which the role played
by music in these banquets can be observed.
Translation of musical terms is, however, often
rather misleading.

\* \* \* \* \* \* \* \* \* \* \*

373. JAPANESE NATIONAL COMMITTEE OF THE IMC. The Japanese
Music. Tokyo: Japanese National Committee of the
International Music Council, 1967. 115p., music,
illus.
A collection of four short articles on Japanese
music and musical instruments by Koizumi Fumio,
Matsudaira Yoritsune, Mitsukuri Shukichi, and Tanabe
Hisao. See individual authors for annotations.

374. JAPANESE RADIO INSTITUTE and P. COLLAER. "Sixteen Ainu
Songs." Ethnomusicologie 1: 195-205, 1954.
Also appears in Les Colloques de Wegimont: Cercle
International d'études ethno-musicologiques,
p.195-205. Ed. by Paul Collaer. Bruxelles: Elsevier,
1956.
Transcriptions of traditional Ainu songs collected
in Sakhalin and Hokkaido between 1947 and 1951.

375. JOCTELEC [pooud.?] "The Biwa." Chrysanthemum 1(1?)·
472-74, 1881.
Short excerpt from Tachibana Nankei's Saiyûki
(1795-98), which gives an account of a great
Satsuma-biwa player, Ikeda Jinbei, of Kagoshima.

376. JOHNSON, Florence B. A Comparative Study of the Basic
Music Talents of Three Racial Groups-- Chinese,
Japanese, and Part-Hawaiian. M.A.Thesis, Univ. of
Hawaii, 1933. NE

377. JOHNSON, Irmgard. "The Role of Amateur Participants in
the Art of Nô in Contemporary Japan." Asian
Music 13(2): 115-33, 1982.
Discussion of the important role that non-profes-
sional students play in sustaining the nô
theater in economic and social terms. Describes the
structure and aims of student recitals. There are
problems, however, in the author's explanations of
both Japanese terms and the musical characteristics
of nô chant.

378. JOLY, H.L. "Random Notes on Dances, Masks, and the Early
Forms of Theatre in Japan." Transactions and
Proceedings on the Japan Society, London. 11:
28-74, 1914.

Survey of the major dance and theater forms of Japan touching upon kagura, bugaku, kabuki, bunraku, nô, and the respective masks used.

379. JONES, Stanleigh H. "Experiment and Tradition: New Plays in the Bunraku Theatre." Monumenta Nipponica 36: 113-31, 1981.
Discussion of three new plays dated from the 1950's: Meiji Tennô ("Emperor Meiji"), Okichi Tsurumatsu Shimoda shigure ("Shimoda Showers-- The Love of Ôkichi and Tsurumatsu") and Nezumi no Sôshi ("The Tale of the Rats").

380. _____. "The Noh Plays Obasute and Kanehira." Monumenta Nipponica 23: 261-85, 1963.
Translations of two nô plays.

381. _____. "Puccini Among the Puppets: Madame Butterfly on the Japanese Puppet Stage." Monumenta Nipponica 38(2): 163-74, 1983.
Second-hand description of the first performance in 1956 of an adaptation of Puccini's Madama Butterfly on the bunraku stage, which does not include details about the music of the performance other than the fact that a single violin was also used for accompaniment.

382. JUNKER VON LANGEGG, Ferdinand Adalbert, trans. "Die Musikfolter Akoya's; Eine Episode aus den Chroniken des Helmkrieges von Dan-no-Ura." Das Magazin für die Literatur der In- und Auslandes 57: 493-98, 512-15, 1888 (Dresden).
A translation, in story form, of the Akoya no koto-zeme ("Music Torture of Akoya") scene from the kabuki play Dan-no-ura kabuto gunki ("Battle of Dan-no-ura"), written by Bunkôdô.

383. _____, trans. Vasallentreu (Chiu-shin-gura-no-bu). Leipzig: 1880. x, 320p.
German rendition of Kanadehon Chûshingura, in story form .

\* \* \* \* \* \* \* \* \* \*

67

384. KAEMPFER, Engelbert. History of Japan. 2 vols.
London, 1727. Trans. by J.G. Scheuchzer.
Reprint in 3 vols. Glasgow, 1906. Facsimile version
of the original 1727 edition, Kyoto, 1929.
Contains some ethnographic accounts of the music of
17th-century Japan. Extracts quoted in Time, Place
and Music: An Anthology of Ethnomusicological Observation c.1550 to c.1800, p.151-54. Ed. by Frank
Harrison. Amsterdam: Frits Knuf, 1973.

385. KAKINOKI Gorô. "A Method for Comparative Analysis of
Japanese Folk Melody by Structural Formulae."
Asian Music 6(1-2): 60-87, 1975 [Perspectives on
Asian Music: Essays in Honor of Dr. Laurence E.
Picken].
Describes a method of abstracting functional unit
stereotype melodic formulas from folk melodies, and
representing them graphically to facilitate comparison. Includes explanation of concepts and symbols,
musical examples with comparative analysis, and
classification of various Japanese folk song
melody-types.

386. _____. "Music Analysis of a Traditional Song: Meaning
and Function of 'Kobushi'." Ongaku Gaku 21(2):
78-88, 1975. graphs, music.
Attempt to elucidate the meaning and function of
kobushi (melismatic ornamentations) in traditional Japanese vocal music by analyzing the
nagauta piece Ninin-Wankyû as performed by
Yoshizumi Jikyô and Yoshizumi Ijûrô.

387. _____. "Regional Folk Song Styles in Japan and Some
Parallels in Indonesian Songs." In Preservation
and Development of the Traditional Performing Arts
[Report of ISCRCP 1980]. p.109-28. Tokyo: Tokyo
National Research Institute of Cultural Properties,
1981.
Examination of Japanese folk song style, with a
comparison to scale structure of certain traditional
Indonesian songs.

388. KAKIUCHI Yukio. "The Traditions of Gidayû-bushi: A
Study and Comparative Analysis of Okuri in Ehon-
Taikôki 10-Danme, Amagasaki no Dan." In Pre-
servation and Development of the Traditional Per-
forming Arts [Report of ISCRCP 1980], p.181-203.
Tokyo National Research Institute of Cultural

68

Properties, 1981.
Comparative analysis of 14 versions of the okuri
section in Amagasaki no Dan performed by different tayû (gidayû-bushi singers).

389. KALVODORA, Dana. "Gagaku." New Orient 6(1): 9-10,
February 1967. NE

390. KAMEI Takayoshi. ed. Heique Monogatari. ⌊facsimile⌋
Tokyo: Yoshikawa Kôbun-Kan, 1969. 408p. plus 6p.
(Table of contents).
Facsimile edition of the Heike Monogatari (The
Tale of Heike; Amakusa version of the Kirishitan
Edition) in Roman script.

391. KAMISANGÔ Yûkô. "Music as One Element in an
Integrated Art Form." In Proceedings of the Second
Asian Pacific Music Conference [Taipei 1976],
p.34-38. Seoul: Cultural and Social Centre for the
Asian and Pacific Region, 1977.
Outline of several chracteristics of Japanese music,
stressing the importance of language and texts, and
the role of music as a single element in the
"integral" stage arts of nô, bunraku and
kabuki.

392. _____. "Traditional Elements in the Compositions of
Miyagi Michio." In Preservation and Development of
the Traditional Performing Arts [Report of ISCRCP
1980], p.143-47. Tokyo: Tokyo National Research
Institute of Cultural Properties, 1981.
Analysis of modern koto music pieces by Miyagi
Michio (1894-1956).

393. KANAI Kikuko. "The Folk Music of the Ryukyus." Journal
of the International Folk Music Council 7: 17-19,
1955.
Introduces the traditional music of the Ryukyu
Islands or Okinawa. Stresses the importance of
Okinawan culture in relation to Japanese culture.

394. KANAZAWA Masakata. "Japan." In Harvard Dictionary of
Music, p.431-35. Edited by Willi Apel. Cambridge,
MA: Harvard Univ. Press, 1969.
Gives a short historical survey of Japanese music.
Materials, including examples given, are out-of-date
and rather inadequate.

395. ____. "Music since 1868; 1. Western Music and
Japan" [Part of Entry "Japan"]. In New Grove
Dictionary of Music and Musicians 9: 549-50.
London; Macmillan, 1980.
Brief outline of the introduction of Western music
into Japan after the Meiji Restoration and composi-
tion in Japan since 1945.

396. KANDA Takahira. "On Some Copper Bells." Transactions
of the Asiatic Society of Japan 4: 29-33, 1876.
Brief account of ancient Japanese temple bells.

397. KANETSUNE Kiyosuke and TSUJI Shôichi. Die geschicht-
lichen Denkmäler der japanischen Tonkunst,
(Saibara). Tokyo: Nanki Music-Bibliothek, 1930. 57p.
[Text in Japanese 16p., in German, 10p.]
Scores (five-line staff) of six saibara pieces
and brief explanatory notes. The first volume in a
planned series on Japanese court music in staff
notation, entitled Nippon ongaku shûsei in
Japanese, that was however never completed.

398. KARUW, Utto. "Utagaki-Kagahi: Ein Beitrag zur Völkskunde
und Religionsgeschichte Altjapan." Monumenta
Nipponica 5(2): 2-45 [287-331], December 1942.
Study of an ancient fertility rite called uta-
gaki or kagai, in which singing and dancing
played an important role. The religious origins,
etymology, history, and remnant practices are
discussed in detail.

399. KÁRPÁTI János. Kelet zenéje [Music of the East].
Budapest: Zenemükiadó, 1981. 327p., music, illus.,
bibliog., discog., index, map and glossary.
Survey of the musical cultures of Asia, with
sections on Japanese religious music, court music,
and music theaters.

400. ____. "Tonality in Japanese Court Music." Studia
Musicologica 25: 171-82, 1983.
Discussion on the tonality-types to be observed in
gagaku based on the author's knowledge of
European-language materials on the subject and his
study trip made to Japan in 1978. Lack of knowledge
of Japanese sources results in some
oversimplification.

401. KATAOKA Gidô. "Cérémonies musicales du Shinto

70

Japonais." In <u>Encyclopédie</u> <u>de</u> <u>musiques</u> <u>sacrées</u>.
Ed. by Jacques Porte. 1: <u>Le</u> <u>Sacré</u> <u>en</u>
<u>Extrême-Orient</u>, <u>Méditerranée</u>, <u>Afrique</u> et
<u>Amérique</u>, p.275-90. Paris: Labergerie, 1968.
Introduction to the <u>mikagura</u> tradition and its
repertoire.

402. _____. "Die Entwicklung der japanischen Musik." In
<u>Almanach, Offizielles Program der Berliner</u>
<u>Festwochen</u>, September 1965.
Short essay discussing the historical outline and
characteristics of Japanese music.

403. _____. "Miyagi, Michio." <u>Die</u> <u>Musik</u> <u>in</u> <u>Geschichte</u> <u>und</u>
<u>Gegenwart</u> 9: 387-88. Kassel: Bärenreiter, 1961.
Biographical notes on a well-known <u>sôkyoku</u>
performer-composer of modern Japan, and a list of
his works.

404. _____. "Musikerziehung in Japan." <u>Neue</u> <u>Zeitschrift</u> <u>für</u>
<u>Musik</u> 116(7): 410-12, 1955.
The sixth of the series "Musikerziehung im Ausland."
Describes traditional Japanese music and Western
music and their contrasting education systems in
Japan.

405. _____. "Shômyô." <u>Die</u> <u>Musik</u> <u>in</u> <u>Geschichte</u> <u>und</u>
<u>Gegenwart</u> 12: 643-49. Kassel: Bärenreiter, 1965.
Brief introduction to <u>shômyô</u>, dealing with
its origins, development in Japan, and its present
state.

406. _____. "Tanaka, Shôhei." <u>Die</u> <u>Musik</u> <u>in</u> <u>Geschichte</u> <u>und</u>
<u>Gegenwart</u> 13: 79-80. Kassel: Bärenreiter, 1966.
Brief biographical notes on a Japanese musico-
physicist.

407. _____. "Zeami." <u>Die</u> <u>Musik</u> <u>in</u> <u>Geschichte</u> <u>und</u> <u>Gegenwart</u>
14: 1032-35. Kassel: Bärenreiter, 1968.
Biographical notes on a great <u>nô</u> actor,
composer and theorist.

408. KAUFMANN, Walter. "The <u>Mudrâs</u> in <u>Sâmavedic</u> Chant
and Their Probable <u>Relationship</u> to the Go-on Hakase
of the Shômyô of Japan." <u>Ethnomusicology</u> 11
(2): 161-69, 1967.
Hypothesis that the neumes of the Japanese
<u>shômyô</u> (Buddhist chant) notation may have

had their origins in the vedic mudrâs.

409. KEELING, Richard H. Shakuhachi Music of the Kinko
School: Techniques and Melodic Embellishment.
M.A. Thesis, UCLA, 1975. NE

410. KEENE, Donald. "The Awaji Puppet Theatre of Japan." In
Essays on Asian Theatre, Music and Dance. New
York; The Performing Arts Program of the Asia
Society, 1973-74. Printed on one sheet.
Brief introduction to the Awaji Ningyô Za.

411. _____. Bunraku: The Art of the Japanese Puppet
Theatre.Tokyo: Kodansha, 1965, 303p. Revised
paperback edition, 1973. 88p.
Bunraku theatergoer's companion. Concise, yet pene
trating text about the history, texts and chanters,
the shamisen and its players, together with the
puppets and the operators. Numerous photographs,
list of plays, bibliography and index are also
included.

412. _____. Chushingura: The Treasury of Loyal
Retainers. New York: Columbia Univ. Press, 1971.
xiv, 183p.
Translation of the well-known puppet play by Takeda
Izumo, Miyoshi Shôraku and Namiki Senryû.

413. _____. Four Major Plays of Chikamatsu. New York:
Columbia Univ. Press, 1961. 220p.
Introduction to Chikamatsu Monzaemon (1653-1725) and
his jôruri (puppet plays), and a translation
of his Sonezaki shinjû (The Love Suicides at
Sonezaki),Kokusen'ya kassen (The Battles of
Coxinga), Nebiki no kadomatsu (The Uprooted
Pine), and Shinjû Ten no Amijima (The Love
Suicides at Amijima).

414. _____. Nô: The Classical Theatre of Japan. Tokyo:
Kodansha, 1966. 311p.
Detailed study of the history and performance
practice of nô and kyôgen, copiously
illustrated with more than 400 plates. Includes a
sono-sheet recording with excerts from the nô
play Funa-Benkei.

415. _____, ed. Twenty Plays of the Nô Theatre. New
York: Columbia Univ. Press, 1970. 336p.

Contains translations of the nô plays Matsu-
kaze, Motomezuka, Kayoi Komachi, Sekidera Komachi,
Nishikigi, Semimaru, Obasute, Hanjo, Ashikari,
Shôkun, Nonomiya, Kanawa, Yôkihi, Yugyôyanagi,
Dôjôji, Seiôbo, Kanehira, Ohara Gokô, Tori-
oi-bune, and Tanikô.

416. _____. World within Walls: Japanese Literature of the
Pre-Modern Era 1600-1867. New York: Holt, Rinehart
and Winston, 1976. xiii, 606p.
Primarily a study of Japanese literature during the
Edo period. Five chapters concerning drama, however,
explain the background of kabuki and ningyô-
jôruri.

417. KENNY, Don. A Guide to Kyôgen. Tokyo: Hinoki
Shoten, 1968. 303p.
Synopses of 257 plays in alphabetical order.

418. _____. On Stage in Japan: Kabuki, Bunraku, Noh,
Gagaku. Tokyo: Shufunotomo Sha, 1974. 184p.
illus., biblio.
A playgoer's manual containing brief information on
the gagaku stage; directory of the theaters in
Tokyo, Kyoto, Nara, and Osaka; glossary of Japanese
terms of performing arts as well as the titles of
standard repertoire.

419. KIKKAWA Eishi. "The Dual Personality of Jiuta: Sobriety
and Humor." Trans. by John Tedford. Hogaku 1(1):
9-19, Spring 1983.
Short article dealing with the character of Edo-
period jiuta-sôkyoku, describing in some
detail certain performance practices adopted by the
masters of the art for amusement.

420. _____. "An Introductory Guidance to the Research of the
Shamisen." Tôyô Ongaku Kenkyû 14-15: 52-
63, 1958.
Basic introduction to the shamisen, mentioning
its designations, origin, structure in comparison to
the other three-stringed lutes of Asia, its introduction into Japan and remodeling, tunings, and
manner of performance.

421. _____. 'Traditional Music in the 20th Century.' [Part of
§VII: Music since 1868, sub-entry of "Japan"]  In
New Grove Dictionary of Music and Musicians 9:

552. London: Macmillan, 1980.
Brief survey of movements in traditional music
circles in the 20th century.

422. KIKKAWA Eishi and Leonard HOLVIC. "Letter to the
Editor." Ethnomusicology 12(1): 154-66, 1968.
Comments on W. Adriaansz' "Research into the Chro-
nology of Danmono."

423. KINCAID, Zoc. "Art of Bugaku: World's Oldest Dances."
Eastern Asia 5: 5-15, 1941.
Introduction to Japanese court dance, touching upon
its repertoire, accompanying music, musical instruments, masks, and costumes. Generously illustrated.

424. _____. "Four Drama-Forms of Kabuki," Transactions of
the Asiatic Society of Japan 2nd S.1: 83-99, 1924.
NE

425. _____. Kabuki: the Popular Stage of Japan. London:
Macmillan, 1925. xvi, 385p.
Detailed early study of kabuki and its history,
including a number of historically important old
woodblock-print reproduction and photographs of
actors of the time.

426. KING, E. "Kagura: the Search" In Dance Research
Monograph 1: 75-112. New York, 1971-72. NE

427. KINOSHITA, Eden. "The Construction of the Ryûteki,"
Gagaku Kai 51: 16-32, 1973.
Detailed description of the construction processes
of the ryûteki, the transverse flute used in
the tôgaku style of Japanese court music.
Largely derived from the section on ryûteki
construction in the author's M.A. thesis. See Entry
below.

428. _____. Construction of Ryûteki, Hichiriki, and
Shô: Wind Instruments of Tôgaku in Japanese
Court Music. M.A. thesis, Univ. of Hawaii, 1969.
NE

429. _____. "Construction of Shô." Gagaku Kai 52: 22-
56, 1975.
Detailed description of the construction processes
of the shô, a mouth organ. Based on previous
item.

430. KIRBY, Richard J. "Dazai on Japanese Music." Trans-
     actions of the Asiatic Society of Japan 28: 46-58,
     1900.
     Partial translation of the second book of Keizai-
     roku by Dazai Shundai (1680-1747), which expresses
     the author's view of music, based on Confucian
     philosophy.

431. KIRSTKIN, Lincoln. Bunraku. New York: Dunetz &
     Lovett, 1966. 24p. NE

432. KISHIBE Shigeo. "Bugaku." In Report of the Twelfth
     Congress of International Musicological Society,
     Berkeley, August 21-26, 1977, p.737-39. Kassel:
     Bärenreiter, 1981.
     Paper presented at the roundtable "Court Dance East
     and West." Brief introduction to Japanese court
     dance.

433. _____. "Ethnomusicology in Japan." In Asian Culture
     Quarterly 7(2): 28-37, 1979.
     A brief account of musicological activities in Japan
     today, focusing on the fields of Japanese music
     research and ethnomusicology.

434. _____. 'General' [§I of the entry "Japan"]. In New
     Grove Dictionary of Music and Musicians 9: 505-6.
     London: Macmillan, 1980.
     Short introduction to encyclopedia entry, dealing
     with the chronological divisions of Japanese music
     history, and matters of musical aesthetics.

435. _____. "Japanese Music--Conflict or Synthesis?" World
     of Music 9(2): 11-21, 1967.
     The cause of conflict between traditional music and
     modern Western music in Japan is examined, and
     various attempts to combine or synthesize the two
     are discussed. In English, French, and German.

436. _____. "Means of Preservation and Diffusion of
     Traditional Music in Japan." Asian Music 2(1):
     8-13, 1971.
     Paper presented at a conference held in Berlin,
     1967, by the International Institute for Comparative
     Music Studies and Documentation. A brief survey of
     the state of traditional Japanese music, centering
     on performers, organizations for preservation, and
     the training of musicians.

75

437. _____. "Music Education in the Countries of the Orient: Japan." In Proceedings of a Conference held in Tehran Organized by the Asian Music Circle and the Iranian National Music Committee 7th-12th September, 1967, p.63-65. Berlin: International Institute for Comparative Music Studies and Documentation, 1968.
Some unique aspects of music education in modern Japan.

438. _____. "Music Theater, with Special Reference to Vocal Technique." In Report of the Twelfth Congress of International Musicological Society, Berkeley, August 21-26, 1977, p.660-61. Kassel: Bärenreiter, 1981.
Brief remarks concerning the male style of art (otoko-gei) and the narrative style of vocal music (katari-mono) as the two basic disciplines of the vocal technique used in the traditional Japanese musical theaters.

439. _____. "The Origin of the K'ung-Hou (Chinese Harp)." Tôyô Ongaku Kenkyû 14-15: 1-51, 1958.
English version of the author's article in Japanese entitled "Kugo no engen," which appeared in Kôkogaku Zasshi 39 (3-4): 1954. Study of the origin and diffusion of three types of harp based on historical documentary and iconographical sources. A companion study of the "The Origin of the P'i-p'a."

440. _____. "The Origin of the P'i-p'a." The Transactions of the Asiatic Society of Japan, 2nd Series 19: 259-304, 1940. Revised version of the article "Biwa no engen," which appeared in the Kôkogaku Zasshi 22(10 & 12), 1936.
Discussion of the origin of the short-necked lute of East Asia, with special reference to the five-stringed lute preserved in the Shôsôin Repository of Nara.

441. _____. "The Society for Research in Asiatic Music: Its Aims, Functions and Achievements." Ethnomusicology Newsletter 10: 12-14, 1957.
Introduction to the function and aims of the Tô-yô Ongaku Gakkai. English adaptation by William P. Malm.

442. _____. 'Noh' [Subsection of §III. Theatrical and Courtly

Genres. Part of the entry "Japan"]. In New Grove
Dictionary of Music and Musicians 9: 515-19.
London: Macmillan, 1980.
Outline of nô, under the following headings:
history, stage plan, actors and acting, musical
form, tonal system, rhythm, instruments, and
aesthetics.

443. _____. The Traditional Music of Japan. Tokyo:
Kokusai Bunka Shinkokai, 1966. ix, 57p., illus.
Short introduction to various genres. Originally
published as a booklet attached to the record album
of the same title, Victor (Japan), JL32-34.

444. KITAGAWA Hiroshi and Bruce T. TSUCHIDA, trans. The
Tale of Heike. Foreword by E. Seidensticker.
Tokyo: Univ. of Tokyo Press, 1975. xli, 807p.
Complete translation of Heike Monogatari, a 13th
century epic which was recited by biwa-hôshi,
blind Buddhist monks who accompanied themselves on
the biwa. The text of heikyoku.

445. KITAHARA Michio. "Kayokyoku: An Example of Syncretism
Involving Scale and Mode." Ethnomusicology 10
(3): 271-84, 1966.
Attempt to illustrate the theory of syncretism,
indicating how one type of musical scale is
identified with another in the creation of a style
resulting from acculturation.

446. KITAZAWA Masakuni. "Situation of Creative Art in the
Industrial Society." In Music--East and West:
Report on 1961 Tokyo East-West Music Encounter
Conference, p.178-80. Tokyo: Executive Committee
for 1961 TEWMEC, 1961.
Brief sociological observations on the music-making
scene of Japan in the late 50's.

447. KNOSP, Gaston. "Note sur la musique japonaise." Le
Guide Musical 57(4): 63-65, 1911.
Brief survey of Japanese music and musical scales,
with remarks on the similarity between Japanese and
Gypsy scales.

448. KNOTT, C.G. "Remarks on Japanese Musical Scales."
Transactions of the Asiatic Society of Japan 19
(2): 373-92, 1891.
Critical comment on Francis Piggott's paper on the

music of the Japanese (Entry 657) concerning in particular Piggott's transcription of koto music,
and analysis of its scale and tonality.

449. KOCH, Peter. "Erfahrungen in Japan: Japans Kotosaiten im
Westwind." Musik und Bildung 10(2): 120-21,
1978.
Short note expressing surprise at the overwhelming
domination of Western music in Japanese musical
life.

450. KOIZUMI Fumio. 'Biwa' [Part of §IV. Instruments and
Their Music. Sub-entry of "Japan"]. In New Grove
Dictionary of Music and Musicians 9: 524-26.
London: Macmillan, 1980.
Short description of the biwa and the music
genres in which it is used, including treatment of
gaku-biwa, môsô-biwa, heike-biwa, satsuma-
biwa, chikuzen biwa and biwa in contemporary
music.

451. _____. "Contemporary Music in Occidental Style
and Its Problem in Japan." In The Preservation of
Traditional Forms of the Learned Music of the Orient
and the Occident, p.184-89. Ed. by William Kay
Archer. Urbana, IL: Institute of Communications
Research, Univ. of Illinois, 1964.
Paper read at the International Congress of the IMC
of UNESCO at Tehran during April 6-12, 1961. Deals
with the problems faced by Japanese composers in
blending modern Western musical styles with elements
of traditional music.

452. _____. 'Japanese Folk Music' [Part of §VI. Folk Music.
Sub-entry of "Japan"]. In New Grove Dictionary
of Music and Musicians 9: 540-43. London:
Macmillan, 1980.
Wide-ranging description of Japanese folk music,
dealing with history, warabeuta (children's game
song), min'yô (general term for folk song),
and the music of minzoku-geinô (folk performing arts).

453. _____. "Music Scales in Japanese Music." In Asian
Musics in an Asian Perspective [Report of ATPA
1976], p.73-79. Tokyo: Japan Foundation, 1977.
English version of the author's article entitled
"Theory of Japanese Music" included in Nippon no

78

ongaku: <u>Rekishi</u> <u>to</u> <u>riron</u>, p.73–83. Tokyo:
Kokuritsu Gekijô, 1974.
Argues that Japanese melodies are constructed on one
or a combination of four types of tetrachords. The
author identifies four kinds of musical scales in
traditional Japanese music.

454. _____. 'Popular Music' [Part of §VII. Music since 1960.
Sub-entry of "Japan"]. In <u>New</u> <u>Grove</u> <u>Dictionary</u> <u>of</u>
<u>Music</u> <u>and</u> <u>Musicians</u> 9: 550–52. London: Macmillan,
1980.
Brief history of popular music in Japan after the
Meiji Restoration.

455. _____. "Rhythm in Japanese Folk Music." In <u>The</u>
<u>Japanese</u> <u>Music</u>, pp. 14–34. Tokyo: Japanese
National Committee of the International Music
Council, 1967.
English summary of the author's article "Nippon no
rizumu," <u>Ongaku</u> <u>Geijutsu</u> 20(11): 24–34, 1962.
Elucidates certain rhythmical characteristics found
in traditional Japanese music. Revised and reprinted
in <u>Musical</u> <u>Voices</u> <u>of</u> <u>Asia</u> [Report of ATPA 1978],
p.108–19. Tokyo: Japan Foundation, 1980.

456. _____. "Three Important Aspects in the Training of
Professionals of Japanese Traditional Music."
<u>International</u> <u>Music</u> <u>Education:</u> <u>ISME</u> <u>Year</u> <u>Book</u> 2:
15–16, 1974.
Presents three major curricular problems facing
students majoring in traditional Japanese music in
the modernized school system at Tokyo Geijutsu
Daigaku (Tokyo National University of Fine Arts and
Music).

457. _____. "The Theoretical Elements of Japanese Music."
<u>The</u> <u>East</u> 19(1–2): 25–31, March 1983; 19(3–4):
25–31, May 1983; 19(5–6): 21–25, July 1983.
First three of a planned series of four articles on
the characteristics of Japanese music, cut short by
the author's untimely death. Part 1 "Sound Materials
—the Timbre of the Voices and Musical Instruments
in Japanese Music"; Part 2 "Rhythm—Transitional
Aspects of Music in Time"; Part 3 "Musical Forms."

458. _____. "Towards a Systematization of Japanese Folk
Song." <u>Studia</u> <u>Musicologica</u> 7: 309–13, 1965.
Paper read at the International Folk Music Council

Conference in Budapest in August 1964. Brief summary
of the author's work with Japanese folk song.
Outlines a new system of classification based on
tetrachord structure and rhythmic type, which was
originally published in Japanese, Nihon dentô
ongaku no kenkyû [Study of Traditional Japanese
Music], Tokyo: Ongaku no Tomo Sha, 1958.

459. _____, ed. Warabeuta no kenkyû [Game Songs of
Japanese Children]: Report of a Group-Study on
Warabeuta of Tokyo in 1961, 2 vols. Tokyo: Warabeuta
no Kenkyû Kankôkai, 1969. xi, 565p. illus.,
music.
Volume One consists of comparative scores of game
songs transcribed into staff notation. Most of the
song-texts are translated into English. Volume Two
consists of monographs in Japanese dealing with
various aspects of traditional game songs of
Japanese children.

460. KOIZUMI Fumio and OKADA Kazuo. Gagaku: The Noble Music
of Japan. Göttingen: Institut für den wissenschaftlichen Film, 1974. 97p., bibliog., illus.,
photos. [Publikationen zu wissenschaftlichen Filmen.
Sektion Völkerkunde-Volkskunde, Ergänzungsband 5]
Booklet that accompanies five films on gagaku
and bugaku, Japanese court music and dance, produced by the Encyclopedia Cinematographica Archives.

461. KOIZUMI Fumio, TOKUMARU Yoshihiko and YAMAGUCHI Osamu,
eds. Asian Musics in an Asian Perspective
[Report of ATPA 1976]. Tokyo: The Japan Foundation,
1977. xvi, 375p., illus., music, bibliog., glossary.
Proceedings of "A Week of Asian Traditional
Performing Arts 1976" held in Tokyo during March 27-
April 8, 1976 under the auspices of the Japan
Foundation. Includes several articles and reports
concerning traditional Japanese music and descrip-
tions of Japanese musical instruments.

462. KOJIMA Shin. "Tonale Strukturen und ihr tonsystemati-
scher Zusammenhang im japanischen Volkslied." In
Bericht über den internationalen Musikwissenschaftlichen Kongress Leipzig 1966, p.547-49.
Kassel: Bärenreiter, 1967.
Discusses the three kinds of pentatonic scales and
seven modes of Japan and illustrates their tonal
relationships.

463. KOKUSAI BUNKA SHINKOKAI, ed. The Noh Drama. Tokyo:
     Kokusai Bunka Shinkokai, 1937. 65p.
     Translation of two popular nô plays,
     Hagoromo and Aoi-no-ue.

464. KOMINZ, Laurence. "The Noh as Popular Theater:
     Miyamasu's Youchi Soga." Monumenta Nipponica
     ƆƆ(ƙ)ᵢ ƙƙ1 5Ɔᵢ 197Oᵢ
     Introductory essay and translation of the nô
     play Youchi Soga.

465. _____. "Ya no Ne: The Genesis of a Kabuki Aragoto
     Classic." Monumenta Nipponica 38(4): 387-407,
     1983.
     Outline of the development of the aragoto style
     of kabuki acting, with a translation of the
     early 18th century play Ya no Ne.

466. KOMIYA Toyotaka, ed. Japanese Music and Drama in the
     Meiji Era. Translated by Edward Seidensticker and
     Donald Keene. Tokyo: Obunsha, 1956. 535p. [Japanese
     Culture in the Meiji Era, 3]
     Historical review of the trends and changes in music
     and drama during the Meiji era, 1868-1912, by such
     specialists as Machida Kashô, Furukawa Hisashi,
     Miyake Shûtarô and Toita Yasuji.

467. KOMIYAMA Wataru. "Multiplicity of Vocalization Styles in
     Japanese Musics." In Musical Voices of Asia
     [Report of ATPA 1978], p.120-24. Tokyo: Japan
     Foundation, 1980.
     An attempt to describe the large number of charac-
     teristic vocalization styles used in the major
     genres of traditional Japanese music.

468. KOMPARU Kunio. The Noh Theater: Principles and
     Perspectives. Trans. by Jane Corddry (text) and
     Stephen Comee (plays). New York: Weatherhill, 1983.
     384p.
     English-language edition of the author's book Nô
     e no izanai, published by Tankosha in 1980. The
     author, both a nô performer and architectural
     writer by profession, attempts to analyze nô
     from a modern perspective. Section dealing with the
     music of nô relies on traditional accounts.

469. KRAUS FILS, Alexandre. La Musique au Japon.
     Florence: Imprimerie de l'arte della Stampa, 1878;

2nd ed. 1879. 83p., music, illus.
One of the earliest attempts to describe Japanese
music in a Western language. Consisting of eight
chapters which describe briefly the music in the
life of the Japanese, theaters, musicians, music
systems, and musical instruments. Appendix includes
photographs of 85 items from the Japanese instrument
collection of Kraus Museum.

470. KUBOTA Jun. "Tales about Music." Acta Asiatica 23:
25-41, 1972.
Article on ongaku-setsuwa (quasi-historical
tales dealing with music), including passages from
Kokonchomonjū, Gōdanshō, Kojidan, Jikkin-
shō, Imakagami, Zoku-Kojidan, Tōsai-zuihitsu,
and a number of other Heian, Kamakura, and Muromachi
period sources. Classifies them into four categories
according to subject matter.

471. KUCKERTZ, Joseph, ed. Aussereuropäische Musik.
Kassel: Bärenreiter, 1980. 480p.
Collection of articles in Die Musik in Geschichte
und Gegenwart dealing with geographical regions in
Africa, Asia and the Islamic World, Australia and
Oceania, and America. Includes Hans Eckardt's
article "Japanische Musik" (See Entry 193) under the
title "Japan," but omits articles dealing with
instruments, biographies of musicians and individual
genres.

472. KÜFFNER, J. Japanische Weisen (gesammelt von Ph.
Fr. von Siebold). Leiden, 1836. 6p. Reprint, Vienna,
1874.
Seven Japanese tunes, collected by Philipp Franz von
Siebold during 1823-29. Arranged for the piano.

473. KUMAKURA Isao. "Traditional Performing Arts and the
Modern Age." Acta Asiatica 33: 55-73, 1977.
Study of changes in the traditional performing arts
brought about by the Meiji Restoration, pointing out
the existence of a group of arts that did not suffer
any drastic change and a group that were hard hit by
the loss of their financial basis due to decline in
patronage. Deals centrally with developments in
kabuki, tea ceremony and bunraku.

474. KUNZE, Richard. "Buddhistischer Hymnus von Sainokawara."
Die Wahrheit 7: 8-18, 1906.

Translation of the Sai no kawara wasan, a
Buddhist chant sung in colloquial Japanese. Original
Japanese text is provided in Roman letters.

475. ____. Joruri gozen junidan-zoshi: Fräulein Joruri,
Epos in zwölf Gesängen. Tokyo: 1906, 29p.
Translation of Jôruri jûnidan-zôshi with
an introduction and notes. Original Japanese text is
provided in Roman letters.

476. ____. "Zur volkstümlichen japanischen Lyrik."
Mitteilungen des Seminars für orientalische
Sprachen an den Königlichen Friedlich Wilhelms-
Universität zu Berlin, Pt.1. 5: 29-64, 1902.
Translations of various types of popular songs, both
traditional and contemporary, with introduction and
remarks by the translator. Musical notation is
occasionally included.

477. KURIYAMA Meiken and KOIZUMI Fumio, eds. Shingi-Shingon
shômyô shûsei [Buddhist Chant of Shingi-
Shingon], vol.1. Tokyo: Shingi-shingon shômyô
shûsei kankôkai, 1969. xxviii, 235p.,
neumes and transcriptions.
Anthology of the Shingon Buddhist chants transmitted
in the Shingi school. Traditional notation and transcriptions into five-line staff. Text both in
Japanese and English.

478. KUSANO Taeko. "Unknown Aspects of Korean Influence on
Japanese Folk Music." Yearbook for Traditional
Music 15: 31-37, 1983.
Note on a few folkloric performing arts of Japan,
which might have been influenced by Korean culture
via the Korean delegations of the 17-18th century,
followed by an analysis of the Tôjin odori of
the Suzuka district, Mie Prefecture.

* * * * * * * * * * *

479. LAADE, Wolfgang. "Toru Takemitsu's 'November Steps':
Shakuhachi-Musik und Zen." Indo-Asia 12(1): 84-
86, 1970.
A record review-essay.

480. LACHMANN, Robert. "Musik und Tonschrift des Nô."
Bericht über der I. Musikwissenschaftlichen
Kongress der Deutschen Musikgesellschaft in Leipzig
vom 4. bis 8. Juni 1925, p.80-93. Leipzig:
Breitkopf & Härtel, 1926. illus., music.
Discussion of the notational system and tonal
structure of nô singing, with partial
transcription of the nô play Tomoe.

481. _____. "Orientalische Musik auf Schallplatten."
Musik 24(4): 254-56, 1932.
Comments on a historically important 24-record
collection, Musik des Orients, produced by
Hornbostel, which included within its wide selection
part of a nô play.

482. _____. Posthumous Works I. Zwei Aufsätze: Die Musik
im Volksleben Nordafrika; Orientalische Musik und
Antike. Ed. by E. Gerson-Kiwi. Jerusalem: Magnes
Press, 1974. 59p. illus.
Discussion of the nô theater in comparison
with Greek tragedy.

483. LANDY, Pierre. Musique du Japon (Collection de
l'Institut International d'Etudes Comparatives de la
Musique publiée sous le patronage du Conseil
International de la Musique). Paris: Buchet/
Chastel, 1970. 327p. illus., bibliog., discog.,
glossary.
Reference book for the non-specialist, containing
general remarks on the Japanese concept of music, a
historical outline, musical scales (by Tran Van
Khê), musical instruments, major genres of
Japanese music, and the training and status of
musicians.

484. LANCE, Rudolf. "Japanische Kinderlieder." Mitteilungen
des Seminar für orientalischen Sprachen an der
Königlichen Friedrich Wilhelms-Universität zu
Berlin, Pt.1. 3: 216-31, 1900.
Translation of folk songs sung to and by children,
with comments by the translator. Original text is
given in Roman letters.

485. _____. "Lieder aus der Japanischen Volksschule."
Mitteilungen des Seminars für orientalischen
Sprachen an der Königlichen Friedrich Wilhelms-
Universität zu Berlin, Pt.1. 3: 192-215, 1900.

Translation from Shōgaku shōka ("Elementary
School Songs") compiled by Isawa Shūji and
published circa 1885. Includes music and translator's introduction. Original text is given in
Roman letters.

486. LA RUE, Jan. "Native Music on Okinawa." Musical
Quarterly 32(2): 157-70, April 1946.
Introduction to traditional Okinawan music, musical
instruments, and a few representative songs.

487. _____. 'Okinawa' [Part of §VI. Folk Music. Sub-
entry of the article "Japan"] In New Grove
Dictionary of Music and Musicians 9: 543-48.
London: Macmillan, 1980.
Fairly extensive treatment of the music of Okinawa,
divided into the following sections: traditional
background, instruments and vocal styles, notational
system, the Okinawan renaissance, the kunkunshi
repertory, and melody.

488. _____. The Okinawan Classical Songs: An Analytical and
Comparative Study. Ph.D dissertation, Harvard
Univ., 1952. vii, 260p.
The history and culture of Okinawa; musical
instruments and vocal style; the notational system,
forms, texts, melody, rhythm; the varied unison
style; connections with other oriental styles.
Accompanied by a microfilm of transcriptions of the
greater part of the Okinawan repertoire.

489. _____. "The Okinawan Notation System." Journal of the
American Musicological Society 4(1): 27-35, Spring
1951.
Introduces the kunkunshi notation and examines
its principles and nature.

490. LASKA, Joseph. "Die Musik Japans." Die Musik 20 (3):
179-82, 1927.
Brief introduction to Japanese music with short
notes on the shakuhachi, utai, koto, nagauta,
and jōruri.

491. LEITER, Samuel L. The Art of Kabuki: Famous Plays in
Performance. Berkeley: Univ. of California Press,
1979. 298p.
Introductory essay about the form (kata) of
kabuki,and translations of famous scenes from

such plays as Benten kozô, Sugawara denju
tenarai kagami, Shunkan, and Naozamurai.

492. ____. Kabuki Encyclopedia: An English-Language
Adaptation of 'Kabuki Jiten.' Westport, CT:
Greenwood, 1979. xxxix, 572p. illus.
An adapted translation of Kabuki jiten, edited
by Yamamoto Jirô et al., and published in Japan in
1972.

493. LEROUX, Charles. "La Musique classique Japonaise."
Bulletin de la Société Franco-Japonaise de Paris
19-20: 37-57, June-September 1910.
Describes the gist of the tone system, scales and
modes used in gagaku, as well as musical
notation and twelve pitches. Also includes notation
and transcriptions of Senzai, a kagura
piece, and Mushiroda, a saibara piece.

494. LIEBERMAN, Frederic. Contemporary Japanese Composition, Its Relationship to Concepts of Traditional
Oriental Music. M.A. Thesis, Univ. of Hawaii,
1965. vii, 161p.
Attempts to isolate characteristic elements of
Oriental aesthetic morphology and compare their
function in a traditional context with that of
elements in the music of three leading contemporary
Japanese composers. AU

495. ____. "Music in The Tale of Genji." East-West
Center Review 2(1): 1-5, 1965. Reprinted in
Asian Music 2(1): 39-42, 1971.
Essay examining references to music found in The
Tale of Genji, as translated by Arthur Waley.

496. LOEB, David. "An Analytic Study of Japanese Koto Music."
In Music Forum 4: 335-93. Ed. by Felix Salzer.
New York: Columbia Univ. Press, 1976.
Historical and theoretical considerations of
Japanese koto music, and an attempt to apply
Schenkerian linear analysis to Midare and other
compositions.

497. LUBIENSKI, Stephan. "Notes sur la musique japonais."
Revuer des arts asiatiques (Décembre 1927): 231-
34.
Cursory note on Japanese music and musical
instruments. Essentially the same content also

appears in "Die Musik in Japan," Musikblätter des Anbruch 9: 273-79, 1927; "La Musique au Japon," Guide du Concert 13: 823-25, 855-57, 877-89, 1926-27; "De Musiek in Japan," De Muziek 4(2): 65-74, (3): 122-128, 1929; and "Sztuka dzwiekow w krainie wschodzacego slonkca," Muzyka 4: 209-13, 472-76, 1927.

* * * * * * * * * * *

498. MABUCHI Usaburo. "Ein japanisches Kinderlied." In Festschrift Walter Wiora, p.552-60. Ed. by Ludwig Finscher and Christoph-Hellmut Mahling. Kassel: Bärenreiter, 1967.
Discussion of the melodic characteristics of Japanese children's game songs in comparison to tunes from other countries.

499. _____. "Zur Phönomen des Melodie-Typus in der japanischen Musik der Edo-Zeit." Osaka kyôiku daigaku kiyô [Memoirs of Osaka Kyôiku Univ.] 1st S. 28(1): 35-44, December 1979. Discussion of the term senritsu-kei ("Melody-type") and its use in regard to the music of 17-18th century Japan.

500. MACHIDA Kashô. "Japanese Music and Dance." In Japanese Music and Drama in the Meiji Era, p.329-448. Ed. by Komiya Toyotaka. Trans. by Edward Seidensticker and Donald Keene. Tokyo: Obunsha, 1956.
Detailed description of the changes and trends in traditional music and dance during the period when Japan was inundated by Western cultural influences.

501. _____. Notes on Japanese Music, with Special Reference to the Album of Japanese Music Compiled by Kokusai Bunka Shinkokai. Tokyo: Kokusai Bunka Shinkokai, 1949. 51p., illus.
Commentary on the history and forms of the major genres of Japanese music, written to accompany an album of Japanese music recordings.

502. _____. (MATIDA Kashô). Odori (Japanese Dance). Tokyo: The Board of Tourist Industry, Japanese

Government Railways, 1938. 70p. [Tourist Library 22]
General survey of Japanese dance, followed by descriptions of kabuki dance and movements towards a new type of dance.

503. MACFARLAND, Alice. "Japanese Music and Western Ears." Contemporary Japan 8(9): 1108-13, November 1939. An American tourist's impressions of the music of East and West.

504. McCLATCHIE, Thomas R.H. trans. Japanese Plays (Versified)...with Illustrations, Drawn and Engraved by Japanese Artists. Yokohama, 1879. 139p. illus. Translations in rhymed verse of six kabuki plays Chûshingura, Kaga sôdô, Amako jûyûshi, Banchô sarayashiki, Saiyûki, and Nikai-gasa.

505. McCONATHY, Osborne. "'Mason Song' in Japan." Music Educators Journal 34: 20-22, September 1937. Short article in essay style on Luther W. Mason and his part in introducing Western music to Japan in the late 19th century. Written by an apparent acquaintance of Mason, it is interesting in that it gives an account of Mason's thoughts at the time.

506. McCULLOUGH, William H. and Helen CRAIG. trans. A Tale of Flowering Fortunes: Annals of Japanese Aristocratic Life in the Heian Period. 2 vols. Stanford, CA: Stanford Univ. Press, 1980. xv,910p. Translation of the Heian-period chronicle Eiga monogatari. In addition to Chapter 17 entitled "Music," there are many other references to music and musicians.

507. McKINNON, Richard N. "The Nô and Zeami." Far Eastern Quarterly 11: 355-61, May 1952. Introductory essay on the characteristics of nô and the ideas of Zeami concerning effectiveness in performance.

508. _____. "Zeami on the Art of Training." Harvard Journal of Asiatic Studies 16 (1-2): 200-25, June 1953. Well-documented account of Zeami's views on the training of actors. Centering on aesthetic problems, there is little treatment of musical topics.

509. MADDEN, Maude. transl. Golden Chopsticks and Other
     Japanese Children's Songs. Sendai: Takeda, 1904.
     30p.
     Translation of 31 traditional game-songs and
     lullabies as well as the national anthem.

510. MAKINO Yoshio. "My Thoughts about the Drama in Japan and
     in England." The Nineteenth Century and After
     72: 1184-201. London, 1912.
     Contains translation of a scene from Gosho-zakura
     horikawa youchi, a kabuki play by Bunkôdô,
     and part of the scene of the execution of the bandit
     Ishikawa Goemon from Sanmon gosan no kiri.

511. MALM, Joyce R. "The World of Japanese Classical Dance."
     World of Music  25(1): 70-79, 1983.
     Outline of the major genres of Japanese dance,
     including gigaku, kagura, bugaku, nô dance,
     kabuki dance and nihon buyô.

512. MALM, William P. "Asian Music in Collegiate Education
     with Special Reference to the Education of Music
     Teachers." In The Future of Music Education: Asian
     Music in the Schools, p.66-71. Ed. by Henry L.
     Cady. Columbus, OH: Ohio State Univ., 1974.
     Paper suggesting a method of imparting knowledge of
     world music to college students. Reference made to
     certain aspects of Japanese festival music called
     matsuri-bayashi, nô drama music, and
     shakuhachi music.

513. _____.'Bunraku' [Part 3 of §III. Theatrical and Courtly
     Genres. Sub-entry of the article "Japan"]. In New
     Grove Dictionary of Music and Musicians 9: 519-22.
     London: Macmillan, 1980.
     Short survey of the history and musical aspects of
     bunraku.

514. _____. "Chinese Music in the Edo and Meiji Period in
     Japan." Asian Music 6 (1-2): 147-72, 1975 [Per-
     spectives in Asian Music: Essays in Honor of Dr.
     Laurence E. R. Picken].
     Preliminary report of research on the
     minshingaku tradition in Japan and the intro-
     duction of sources.

515. _____. "Edo Festival Music and Pantomime." In Essays
     on Asian Music and Theater. New York: The

Performing Arts Program of the Asian Society,
1971–72.
Brief introduction to matsuri-bayashi and
sato-kagura.

516. _____. "The Eight Day Festival on Miyakejima." Journal
of American Folklore 75 (301): 195–205, 1963.
Ethnographic report of Yôka-matsuri ("Eight
Day Festival") on Miyakejima, a small volcanic
island in the Pacific Ocean, January 1957.

517. _____. "Four Seasons of the Old Mountain Woman: An
Example of Japanese Nagauta Text Setting."
Journal of the American Musicological Society 31
(1): 83–117, 1978.
Analysis of Shiki no yamanba, a classical
nagauta piece composed by Kineya Kangorô
(1829–77).

518. _____. "An Introduction to Taiko Drum Music in the
Japanese Nô Drama." Ethnomusicology 4(2): 75–
78, 1960.
Discussion of the system of rhythmic patterns found
in Konparu school taiko music.

519. _____. "Japanese Music: A Brief Survey." World of
Music 20(3): 64–68, 1978.
Lecture delivered in the 1974 Musicultura I at
Breukelen, the Netherlands. With summaries in French
and German.

520. _____. "Japanese Music and Its Relations to Other
Musical Traditions." World of Music 25(1): 5–15,
1983.
Outline of the remnants of mainland Asian musics
that can be seen in Japanese gagaku.

521. _____. Japanese Music and Musical Instruments.
Rutland, VT & Tokyo: Tuttle, 1959. 299p., music,
illus., bibliog., discog., index and glossary.
Standard reference book in English on Japanese
music. Informative and entertaining, but requires
corrections of numerous flaws, being mostly based on
secondary sources and works up to the 1950's.

522. _____. "Japanese Nagauta Music." In Festival of
Oriental Music and the Related Arts, p.33–36. Los
Angeles: Univ. of California Press, 1960.

Brief introduction to nagauta.

523. _____. 'Kabuki' [Part 4 of §III. Theatrical and Courtly
Genres. Sub-entry of the article "Japan"] In New
Grove Dictionary of Music and Musicians 9: 522-24.
London: Macmillan, 1980.
Brief study of kabuki, concentrating on perform-
ing practice and musical structure.

524. _____. 'Kabuki-Musik.' Part of article "Musik." In
Japan-Handbuch, col.1228-34. Ed. by H.
Hammitzsch. Wiesbaden: Franz Steiner, 1981.
Short outline of the history and musical
characteristics of kabuki music.

525. _____. "Layers of Modern Music and Japan." Asian
Music 4(2): 3-6, 1973.
Short paper read at the International Conference on
Japanese Studies held at the Japan P.E.N. Club in
Kyoto, 1972.

526. _____. "The Modern Music of Meiji Japan." In Tradition
and Modernization in Japanese Culture, p.257-300.
Edited by Donald H. Shively. Princeton: Princeton
Univ. Press, 1971.
Discussion of several different kinds of music in
the Meiji period, with an emphasis on school music
and popular music which grew out of the introduction
of Western music in the mid-19th century.

527. _____. "A Musical Approach to Jôruri." In
Chûshingura: Studies in Kabuki and the Puppet
Theatre, p.59-110. Ed. by James Brandon. Honolulu:
Univ. Press of Hawaii, 1982.
Valuable study of the music of jôruri,
centering on the genre gidayûbushi. Based on
contemporary performance practice and the author's
experience in private lessons, it also appends
examples of gidayû-bushi transcribed into
Western notation.

528. _____. "The Musical Characteristics and Practice of the
Japanese Noh Drama in an East Asian Context." In
Chinese and Japanese Music-Drama, p.99-142.
Edited by J. I. Crump and W. P. Malm. Ann Arbor:
Center for Chinese Studies, Univ. of Michigan, 1975.
Examination of rhythmic organization in the nô
drama.

529. _____. "Music Cultures of Momoyama Japan." In
Warlords, Artists, and Commoners, p.163-85.
Ed. by George Elison and Bardwell L. Smith.
Honolulu: Univ. of Hawaii Press, 1981.
Discussion of the variety of music styles and their
respective audiences found in 16th century Japan.
The article deals with gagaku (music for the
nobility), nô (as music for the parvenus),
various religious, theatrical, and foreign musics,
as well as dengaku, furyû and matsuri-
bayashi (music of the commoners).

530. _____. Music Cultures of the Pacific, the Near East,
and Asia. Englewood Cliffs, NJ: Prentice-Hall,
1967, 169p,, music, illus,, bibliog., discog. 2nd
revised ed. 1977, 236p.
Textbook which surveys the basic types of music and
musical instruments found in the major Oriental
civilizations and in the island cultures of the
Eastern hemisphere. The chapter "Northeast Asia and
the Island Countries" includes a brief discussion of
Japanese music.

531. _____. "Music, East Asian." In Encyclopaedia Britannica 15th ed. 12: 669-91. Chicago: Encyclopaedia
Britannica, 1974.
Section IV is a historical survey of Japanese music,
divided into "Music before and through the Nara
period," "The Heian Period," "Kamakura, Muromachi
and Edo Periods," and the "Meiji Period and
Subsequent Music."

532. _____. "Music, Traditional." In Kodansha Encyclopedia
of Japan 5: 284-85. Tokyo: Kodansha International,
1983.
Concise survey of the history of Japanese music is
followed by consideration of features that the
author views as characteristic of traditional music
in general. Lack of detail in the historical outline
is clearly due to space limitations; the second
section is perhaps the more valuable of the two.

533. _____. Nagauta: The Heart of Kabuki Music. Rutland,
VT & Tokyo: Tuttle, 1963. xvi, 239p., illus., music,
bibliog., index and glossary. [Reprint ed. Westport,
CT: Greenwood, 1976. 344p.]
Monograph on nagauta; an expansion of the
authors' doctoral dissertation, Japanese Nagauta

_Music_ (UCLA, 1959. 475p.).
Includes a historical and theoretical outline of
nagauta, description of the music and musical
instruments employed, and a detailed analysis of two
popular nagauta pieces.

534. _____. 'Notational System.' [Sub-entry of the article
"Japan"] In _New Grove Dictionary of Music and
Musicians_ 9: 536-41. London: Macmillan, 1980.
Brief survey of Japanese notational systems, dealing
with vocal music notation and instrumental notation.
Contains a number of inaccuracies: perhaps the most
serious of these is the misreading of the name of a
type of shamisen notation (kosaburo-fu for
kojûrô-fu).

535. _____. "On the Nature and Function of Symbolism  in
Western and Oriental Music," _Philosophy East and
West_ 19(3): 255-456, July 1969.
Attempt to clarify the nature of symbols in music
within the context of comparative aesthetics,
including several examples from Japanese music.
Commentary by Barbara B. Smith, Lee Winters, Peter
Crossley-Holland, and Albert Hofstadter, p.247-63.

536. _____. "Personal Approaches to the Study of Japanese
Music." _Asian Music_ 3(1): 35-39, 1972.
"Confessions of an ethnomusicologist" based upon a
report given several years previously during a
symposium on methodology in ethnomusicology at the
University of Washington.

537. _____. "Practical Approaches to Japanese Music."
_Occasional Papers_ 9: 95-104, 1965 (Center for
Japanese Studies, Univ.of Michigan).Reprinted in
_Readings in Ethnomusicology_, p.353-65. Edited by
D.P. McAllester. New York: Johnson Reprint Corp.,
1971.
Brief discussion of basic concepts in Japanese music
and of its characteristics in comparison with
Western and other musics.

538. _____. "The Rhythmic Organization of Two Drums in the
Japanese No Drama." _Ethnomusicology_ 2(3):
89-95, 1958.
Introduction to the music of the nô drama and
discussion of the rhythmic patterns of the kotsuzumi and ô-tsuzumi drums. Focuses on the

rhythmic progressions, tensions, and rhythmic
cadences.

539. _____. 'Shamisen.'[Part of §IV. Instruments and Their
Music. Sub-entry of the article "Japan"] In New
Grove Dictionary of Music and Musicians 9: 534-36.
London: Macmillan, 1980.
Short survey of the shamisen and musical genres
associated with it. Some oversimplification to be
found in the account was probably due to space
limitations.

540. _____. "Shoden: A Study in Tokyo Festival Music.
When Is Variation an Improvisation?" Yearbook of
the International Folk Music Council 7: 44-66,
1975.
Research into the concepts of variation techniques
in Japanese music, through analysis of various versions of Shôden, a matsuri-bayashi piece.

541. _____. "A Short History of Japanese Nagauta Music."
Journal of the American Oriental Society 80(?):
124-32, 1960.
Discussion of the early forms of shamisen music,
and the rise and development of nagauta through
to the 19th century.

542. _____."Some of Japan's Musics and Musical Principles."
In Musics of Many Cultures: An Introduction,
p.48-62. Ed. by Elizabeth May. Berkeley & Los
Angeles: Univ. of California Press, 1980.
Introduction for Westerners to some of the major
genres of traditional Japanese music and their
principles.

543. _____."The Special Characteristics of Gagaku." KBS
Bulletin on Japanese Culture 99: 1-8, December
1969-January 1970.
Essay centering around the music of gagaku and
its instruments.

544. MAREGA, Mario. trans. "Akogi: Ballata in un Atto di
Seami Motokiyo." Monumenta Nipponica 2(2):
551-72, 1939.
Italian translation of a nô play attributed to
Zeami.

545. _____. trans. "Minase: Nô-gaku della scuola Kita-

94

ryû." Monumenta Nipponica 4(2): 585–99, 1941.
Italian translation of the nô play Minase.

546. _____. trans. "Okina: Il vegliardo." Monumenta
Nipponica 3(2): 610–18, 1940.
Italian translation of the ceremonial nô play
Okina.

547. MARETT, Allan J. "'Banshiki sangun' and 'Shôenraku':
Metrical Structure and Notation of Two Tang-music
Melodies for Flute." In Music and Tradition:
Essays on Asian and Other Musics Presented to
Laurence Picken, p.41–68. Ed. by D.R. Widdess and
R.F. Wolpert. Cambridge: Cambridge Univ. Press,
1981.
Transcriptions of Banshiki sangun and Shôen-
raku from the 10th-century gagaku flute
manuscript Hakuga no fue-fu, together with an
explanation of the principles of its notation.

548. _____. "Differing Notations in Hakuga no fue-fu."
Gagaku Kai 54: 10–13, 1978.
English summary of a study in Japanese on a 10th-
century gagaku flute manuscript, the source-
scores from which it was compiled, and the existence
of differing notational systems in its tablature.

549. _____. Hakuga's Flute-Score: A Tenth-Century Japanese
Source of Tang Music in Tablature. Doctoral dissertation, Cambridge Univ. 1976. iii, 309p.
Detailed study of a 10th-cetury ryûteki
source, including analysis of the tablature notation
and a largely complete transcription.

550. _____. "Interrelationships between Musical and Social
Change in Japanese and Australian Aboriginal
Culture." In Preservation and Development of the
Traditional Performing Arts [Report of ISCRP
1980], p.63–71. Tokyo: Tokyo National Research
Institute of Cultural Properties, 1981.
Argues that distinctive features of present-day
musical forms in Japan reflect the effect of social
change on the musical tradition.

551. _____. "Tunes Notated in Flute-Tablature from a Japanese
Source of the Tenth Century." Musica Asiatica 1:
1–60, 1977.
Study of the ryûteki manuscript, Hakuga no

<u>fue-fu</u>. Includes a largely complete transcription
of the source.

552. MARKHAM, Elizabeth J. <u>Saibara</u>: <u>Japanese</u> <u>Court</u> <u>Songs</u> <u>of</u>
the <u>Heian</u> <u>Period</u>. Cambridge: Univ. of Cambridge,
1983. Vol.1 (text), xx, 411p.; Vol 2 (music), viii,
388p.
A largely unaltered version of the author's doctoral
dissertation, submitted to the Univ. of Cambridge in
1979. A study of the Heian court song genre <u>sai-</u>
<u>bara</u>. Argues that certain <u>saibara</u> pieces share
the same melody with items in the <u>tôgaku</u> and
<u>komagaku</u> repertoires of <u>gagaku</u>, and provides
substantive evidence from early musical manuscripts
and theoretical sources in an effort to demonstrate
that many <u>saibara</u> were sung to a limited number
of melodies. Persuasive but marred by arbitrariness
in its use of source material and a number of other
flaws.

553. MARTINS, Armando. <u>Noh</u>. Tokyo: Maruzen, 1954.
Translation of two <u>nô</u> plays, <u>Kantan</u> and
<u>Hagoromo</u>.

554. MASU Genjirô and TANABE Hideo. <u>Japanese</u> <u>Music</u>.
Tokyo: UNESCO Nippon, 1953. 78p.(English text); 56p.
(Japanese text), illus., music.
Consists of two parts: Pt.1 (by Tanabe), entitled
"The Character of Japanese Music," and Pt.2 (by
Masu), entitled "Japanese Music and Japanese Life,"
which is in reality a cursory description of repre-
sentative genres of traditional Japanese music.
Originally accompanied a record album (Columbia
A2001-2007).

555. MASUMOTO Kikuko. "Transmission of <u>Gagaku</u>: Ways of
training the <u>Gagaku</u> Musicians." In <u>Presevation</u>
and <u>Development</u> <u>of</u> <u>the</u> <u>Traditional</u> <u>Performing</u> <u>Arts</u>
[Report of ISCRCP 1980], p.205-15. Tokyo: Tokyo Na-
tional Research Institute of Cultural Properties,
1981.
Description of the practice methods and traditional
learning processes of <u>gagaku</u>.

556. MATISOFF, Susan. <u>The</u> <u>Legend</u> <u>of</u> <u>Semimaru</u>: <u>Blind</u>
<u>Musician</u> <u>of</u> <u>Japan</u>. New York: Columbia Univ. Press,
1978. xi, 290p.
Study of the growth of the stories surrounding

the figure of Semimaru, a legendary biwa-
playing blind musician of the mid-Heian period.
Translates important literary sources associated
with Semimaru, including two nô (Semimaru
and Ausaka monogurui) and one jôruri by
Chikamatsu (Semimaru). References to music are
made almost exclusively to secondary sources,
especially the works of Tanabe Hisao.

557. MATSUDAIRA Yoritsune. "Establishment of Gagaku." In
The Japanese Music, p 35-38. Tokyo: Japanese
National Committee of the International Music
Council, 1967.
Brief note concerning tonal characteristics of
gagaku.

558. MATSUHARA Iwao. "Folk-Songs: The Voice of Common
Humanity." Oriental Economist 26: 148-49, 1958.
Very brief discussion on emotion and thought
expressed in verses of Japanese folk-songs.

559. MATSUMAE Norio. "Research on the Attitude of the
Japanese People towards Their Cultural Tradition:
Music." In Report on Traditional Forms of Culture
in Japan, p.106-18. Tokyo: Asian Cultural Center
for UNESCO, 1975.
Survey of the general public's attitude towards
traditional music in contemporary Japan, and
problems of the preservation and diffusion of
traditional music in terms of music education.

560. _____. "A Survey on Recent Activities Related to
Traditional Culture: Music." In Report on Traditional Forms of Culture in Japan, p.36-45. Tokyo:
Asian Cultural Center for UNESCO, 1975.
Study on the Japanese people's participation in
traditional music based on several surveys (1967-
72). Discusses trends in the attitude of the general
public towards traditional music.

561. MATSUNAGA Susumu. "The Evolution of Samisen Music."
Contemporary Japan 3(1): 105-13, 1934.
Discussion of the history of shamisen and the
various genres of shamisen music.

562. MATSUYAMA Yoshio. Studien zur Nô-Musik: Eine
Untersuchung des Stückes "Hagoromo" (das Feder-
gewand). Hamburg: Karl Dieter Wagner, 1980. 407p.

Detailed study of the history and music of nô,
dealing in particular with melody and rhythm of
yôkyoku (vocal music of nô), and hayashi (instrumental music). Gives substantial treatment of the play Hagoromo.

563. MAY, Elizabeth. "Encounters with Japanese Music in Los
Angeles." Western Folklore 17(3): 192-95, 1958.
Short description of the author's contacts with Japanese music as it was performed by young Japanese-
Americans in Los Angeles. Some unfortunate printing
errors on p.194 make this page difficult to under-
stand.

564. _____. The Influence of the Meiji Period on Japanese
Children's Music. Berkeley & Los Angeles: Univ. of
California Press, 1963. x, 95p., bibliog., illus.,
music.
Outgrowth of the author's doctoral dissertation,
Japanese Children's Music Before and After Contact
with the West. UCLA, 1958. Study of music
education in Japan during the Meiji period. Beginning with an examination of traditional children's
game songs and music education in pre-Meiji Japan,
the introduction of Western music and formation of
shôgaku shôka (school songs) are discussed
in detail. Numerous examples given in staff
notation.

565. _____. "The Influence of the Meiji Period on Japanese
Children's Music." Journal of Research in Music
Education 13: 110-20, 1965.
Short account of the influence of Western music on
Meiji-period Japanese music; based on the author's
doctoral dissertation (See previous entry).

566. _____. "Japanese Children's Folk Songs Before and After
Contact with the West." Journal of the International Folk Music Council 11: 59-65, 1959.
Brief look at Japanese children's folk songs,
warabeuta, and examination of the works of Isawa
Shûji (1851-1917) and his Music Study Committee
during the early years of the Meiji period.

567. MAYEDA Akio. "Geschichtlichkeit der japanischen
Musik--im Spiegel der Sprache--." Der Musik-
forschung 35(4) Supplement: 32-41, 1982.
Philosophical examination of a number of issues

concerning the possibilities of the establishment
of an authentic history of Japanese music and its
relevance in a global perspective.

568. MERSMANN, Hans. "Notizen von einer Japanreise."
Musica 11(12): 693-701, 1957.
Impressions of a noted German musicologist who
visited Japan in May 1957

569. MEYNERT, Monika. "Japanische Impressionen." Melos 1
(Januar-Februar 1972): 19-22.
Comments on the position of the avantgarde in the
music life of Japan and problems faced by Japanese
composers in the field.

570. MIGITA Isao, ed. The First Song Book of Nippon.
Tokyo: Kawai Gakufu, 1970. 185p.
Collection of 36 folk songs of Japan, arranged with
piano accompaniment by Komori Akihiro and Shimizu
Osamu. Explanatory notes and translation of the
song-texts by the editor.

571. MIHO Mikitarô. "Gramophones and Record Music in
Japan." Contemporary Japan 9: 61-71, 1940.
Short historical account of the introduction of the
gramophone industry into Japan and its development
until 1940.

572. MINAGAWA Tatsuo. "Japanese Noh Music." Journal of the
American Musicological Society 10(3): 181-200,
1957.
Paper read at the AMS annual meeting of 1957. Introduction to nô with detailed explanation of the
music system of this performing art, based on the
Kanze school practice.

573. MINAKAWA Masaki. Four Nô-Plays. Tokyo: Sekibun-
dô, 1934. 70p.
Translation of Kumasaka, Yamanba, Kayoi-Komachi,
and Hachi no ki.

574. MITA Setsuko. A Comparative Study of the Preparation
of School Music Teachers in Japan and the United
States. Doctoral dissertation, Michigan State
Univ., 1957. 281p.
Comparison of the college training of secondary
school teachers in Japan and the United States.
Includes brief history and evaluation of both

systems.

575. MITSUKURI Shukichi. "Japanese Scales and Their Harmonic
     Treatment." In The Japanese Music, p.1-13.
     Tokyo: Japanese National Committee of the
     International Music Council, 1967.
     Consists of three short papers presented on earlier
     occasions. Proposes a new system for the harmonic
     treatment of Japanese melodies, which was explored
     by the author as a composer.

576. MIWA Reitarô, trans. "Asagao's Adventures." Far
     East 1(6): 25-30; (7): 25-27, 1896.
     Translation of Shô utsushi asagao-banashi, a
     jôruri play by Yamada no Kagashi.

577. ____. "Masa-oka, the Loyal Nurse." Far East 1(4):
     22-25; (5): 26-29, 1896.
     Translation of Meiboku sendai hagi, a jô-
     ruri and kabuki play by Matsu Kanshi.

578. MIYAGI Mamoru. "Renewing the Musical Language--An
     Eastern View." In Music--East and West: Report on
     1961 Tokyo East-West Encounter Conference, p.147-
     51. Tokyo Executive Committee for 1961 East-West
     Encounter, 1961.
     The personal approach of a composer-performer toward
     koto music.

579. MIYAKE Shûtarô. Kabuki Drama, 5th ed. Tokyo:
     Japan Travel Bureau, 1954. 126p., illus., bibliog.
     Guide book for foreigners on how to appreciate
     kabuki drama.

580. MIZLER, Lorenz. "Abbildung und kurze Erklärung der
     musikalischen Instrumenten der Japoneser." In
     Mizlers Musikalische Bibliothek. Vol.1, pt.1,
     p.160-68. Leipzig: Mizlerischen Bücher, 1746.
     Brief explanatory notes for thirteen illustrations
     of Japanese musical instruments. The date of this
     source makes it of historical importance.

581. MOREAUX, Serge. "La musique japonaise." In La musique
     des origines à nos jours, p.446-54. Edited by
     Norbert Dufourcq. Paris: Librarie Larousse, 1946.
     General survey of Japanese music and musical
     instruments.

582. MORELL, Robert E. "Passage to India Denied: Zeami's Kasuga Ryûjin." Monumenta Nipponica 37(2): 178-200, Summer 1982.
English translation of Zeami's Kasuga Ryûjin ("The Dragon God of Kasuga") with an introduction examining its literary background in detail.

583. MORICHINI, Giuseppe. '§1. Teatro.' Sub-entry of Giappone (Nihon)." In Encyclopedia dello Spettacolo, p.1228-48. Roma: Le Maschere, 1958.
A survey of the traditional theatrical arts of Japan. Kagura, gigaku, bugaku, ennen-mai, nô, kabuki and ningyô-jôruri are concisely described with numerous illustrations.

584. MORITA Minoru. "An Ancient Style Song in Ennen Festival of Obasama." In Preservation and Development of the Traditional Performing Arts [Report of ISCRCP 1980], p.47-54. Tokyo: Tokyo National Research Institute of Cultural Properties, 1981.
Study of songs accompanying dance performed during the Ennen Festival of Obasama, Miyagi Prefecture.

585. MOTOFUJI, Frank Toshiyuki. A Study of Narukami: An Eighteenth-Century Kabuki Play. Doctoral dissertation, Stanford Univ., 1964. 238p.
Includes translation of Narukami, with a discussion of its author, sources and characteristics.

586. MÜLLER, [Friedrich W. K.] "Einige Notizen über die Japanische Musik." Mittheilungen der Deutschen Gesellschaft für Natur- und Völkerkunde Ostasiens 1(6): 13-31; (8) 41-48; (9): 19-35, 1873-76.
Fairly detailed description of Japanese music theory and instruments, though rather outdated. Contains transcriptions of the kokyû pieces Fujiyu, the gagaku piece Gojôraku and the gekkin piece Manpan ryûsei.

587. _____. "Ethnologische Mitteilungen aus Japan. 2: Ueber die seit kurzem in der ostasiatischen Abteilung aufgestellte grosse japanische Trommel." Zeitschrift für Ethnologie 38: 947-50, 1906.
Notes on a replica dadaiko (large gagaku drum) made for exhibition at the Berlin Museum für Völkerkunde.

101

588. _____. trans. "Ikkaku Sennin: Eine mittelalterliche
japanische Oper, transkribiert und übersetzt." In
Festschrift für Adolf Bastian zu seinem 70
Geburtstage gewidmet von seinen Freunden und
Verehren, p.513-37. Berlin: Dietrich Reimer, 1896.
Early translation, with notes, of the nô play
Ikkaku Sennin. Parallel text, romanization of
the Japanese with German translation.

589. MÜLLER, Gerhild. Kagura: Die Lieder der
Kagura-Zeremonie am Naishidokoro. Wiesbaden:
Harrassowitz, 1971. 196p.
Detailed study of the sacred kagura of the
imperial court that includes an annotated
translation of the text of the kagura songs, and
a discussion of the historical development of the
kagura ceremonies. Based on the author's
doctoral dissertation Kagura...Naishidokoro,
Johann Wolfgang Goethe Univ., 1969.

590. MUELLER, Jacqueline, trans. "The Two Shizukas. Zeami's
Futari Shizuka." Monumenta Nipponica 36:285-
90, 1981.
Introduction to and translation of this nô
play of the 'woman' category composed by Zeami.

591. MURAKAMI, Upton. A Spectator's Handbook of Noh.
Tokyo: Wanya Shoten, 1963. 98p., illus.
Guidebook to the nô theater for the novice,
with English summaries of 90 nô plays. Illustrated
with numerous monochrome photographs.

592. MURAOKA Noriichi. "Music (Japanese)." In Encyclopaedia
of Religion and Ethics 9: 48-51. Edinburgh: T. &
T. Clark, 1917.
Brief introduction to Japanese music, touching upon
its origin and history, musical instruments and
general characteristics.

593. MURATA Yoko. "The Outline of the History of Japanese
Music." Geijutsu to shimpi [Ars et Mystica] 15:
58-65, 1965.
Incomplete chronological table covering the period
from ancient times until 1660. The combination of
numerous mistakes with an almost unreadable English
text makes it difficult to use.

594. MUSCHG, Adolf. "Das japanische Theater." In Das

Atlantisbuch des Theaters, p.905-19. Ed. by M.
Hürlmann. Zürich: Atlantis, 1966.
Chapter on Japanese theater included in a volume on
the theater of the world. Contains sections on
nô and kyôgen, bunraku, kabuki, and
modern theater.


\* \* \* \* \* \* \* \* \* \* \*


595. NAKAMURA Yasuo. Noh: the Classical Theater. Trans.
by Don Kenny. Introduction by Earle Ernst. New York,
Tokyo & Kyoto: Walker & Weatherhill, 1971. 248p.
Generously illustrated introductory study of
nô, dealing with its history, present state,
and characteristics as a stage art.

596. NATIONAL THEATRE OF JAPAN. National Theatre of
Japan. Tokyo: National Theatre of Japan, 1970.
88p., illus.
Brochure introducing the national theatre
(Kokuritsu gekijô), the first state-operated
theater in Japan, which was inaugurated in 1966 for
performance of the traditional performing arts.

597. NATTIEZ, Jean-Jacques. "The Rekkukara of the Ainu
(Japan) and the Katajjaq of the Inuit (Canada): A
Comparison." World of Music 15(2): 33-44, 1983.
Consideration of the possibilities of the study of
two "throat-games," the rekkukara of the Ainu
and the katajjaq of the Inuit (Canadian Eskimo),
as evidence for the existence of a circumpolar music
culture.

598. NEARMAN, Mark J. "Kakyô: Zeami's Fundamental Principles of Acting." Monumenta Nipponica 37(3):
333-74, Autumn 1982; 37(4): 459-966, Winter 1982;
38(1): 49-71, Spring 1983.
Annotated translation of Zeami's Kakyô (1424),
with introduction and copious commentary.

599. _____. "Zeami's Kyûi: A Pedagogical Guide for
Teachers of Acting." Monumenta Nipponica 33(3):
299-332, 1978.
Examination of Kyûi, one of the Zeami's

important treatises, with a new translation.

600. NELSON, Steven G. Musical Notations of Japan. Tokyo:
Research Archives for Japanese Music of Ueno Gakuen
College, 1983. v, 16 (English text), 8 (photos), v,
15 (Japanese text by Fukushima Kazuo).
Descriptive catalogue of the 8th exhibition of the
above-mentioned archives, with text in English by
Nelson and Japanese by Fukushima. Includes 60
examples of materials on Japanese music which form a
representative selection of traditional musical
notations, ranging from an 8th century biwa
tablature to a 19th-century tablature collection of
imported English military tunes. Headed by a brief
account of the history of musical notations in
Japan. AU

601. NGUYEN Thi Lan. "Koto Music." Asian & Pacific
Quarterly of Cultural and Social Affairs 6(2): 43-
54, 1974. (Seoul: Cultural and Social Centre for the
Asian and Pacific Region).
Outline of the history of the koto and its
music, with remarks on Japanese music teaching. An
article for the non-specialist.

602. NICKSON, Noel. "Japanese Music in Western Music
Education." The Australian Journal of Music
Education 23: 33-38, 1978.
Argument for the inclusion of Japanese music in
Western music education. Introductory notes on
selected source materials are attached.

603. _____. "Shêng and Shô: Traditional Mouth Organs of
China and Japan." In Challenge in Music
Education, p.376-80. Nedlands, Western Australia:
Univ. of Western Australia Press, 1976.
Gives a concise organological description of the two
mouth organs and related instruments, and a short
description of the history of this type of
instrument in East Asia.

604. NIPPON GAKUJUTSU SHINKOKAI. Japanese Noh Drama, 3
vols. Tokyo: Nippon Gakujutsu Shinkôkai, 1955-60.
Vol.1, 1955, xviii, 192p.; Vol.2, 1959, 190p.;
Vol.3, 1960, 201p.
Introduction to and translation of 30 nô plays
by the Japan Society for the Promotion of Scientific
Research. Vol.1 contains Takasago, Tamura, Sane-

mori, Kiyotsune, Tôboku, Izutsu, Eguchi, Bashô,
Sumidagawa, and Funa-benkei. Vol.2 contains
Tamanoi, Tadanori, Yuya, Kantan, Motomezuka, Aoi
no ue, Settai, Kagekiyo, Momijigari, and
Yamamba. Vol.3 contains Tomoe, Hagoromo,
Matsukaze, Miidera, Sotoba-komachi, Yoroboshi,
Kinuta, Shunkan, Ataka, and Ama.

605. ____. The Noh Drama: Ten Plays from the Japanese.
Rutland, VT & Tokyo: Tuttle, 1976. xvi, 192p.
Identical with Vol.1 of Japanese Noh Drama. See
Entry 604 for details.

606. NIPPON HOSO KYOKAI (NHK), ed. Ainu dentô ongaku
[Traditional Ainu Music] Tokyo: Nippon Hôsô
Shuppan Kyôkai, 1965. 566p., illus., 4 sono-sheets
(17cm-records).
Collection of traditional songs of the Ainu.
Transcriptions into five-line staff are accompanied
with text in Roman letters. Explanatory text by
Tanimoto Kazuyuki is in Japanese.

607. NISHIKAWA Kyôtarô. Bugaku Masks. Trans. by
Monica Bethe. New York and Tokyo: Kodansha International, 1982. 194p., plates, glossary, bibliog.,
and index.
Detailed introduction to the historical background,
types, and technical aspects of the masks worn in
the ancient Japanese dance form bugaku, with
numerous illustrations. Accompanied by an introductory essay by Monica Bethe entitled "The Bugaku
Dance."

608. NOGAMI Toyoichirô. Zeami and His Theories on Nô.
Translated by Matsumoto Ryôzô. Tokyo: Hinoki
Shoten, 1955. 88p.
A concise yet penetrating interpretation of
Zeami's Fûshikaden or Kadensho (See
Entries 109, 117, 692 and 722) by a renowned scholar
of the nô theater.

609. NOGUCHI Yone. "The Blind Musician." The Yôkyokukai
5(6): 1-6, December 1916.
Translation of the nô play Semimaru, which
deals with a legendary blind biwa player.

610. NOMURA Kôichi. "Occidental Music." In Japanese Music
and Drama in the Meiji Era, p.451-507. Edited by

Komiya Toyotaka. Translated by E. Seidensticker and
D. Keene. Tokyo: Obunsha, 1956.
Article dealing with the introduction of Western
music into Japan in the Meiji period, providing
translation of some important source materials.

611. NOMURA Yosio. "Beethoven and Japanese Musicology." In
Bericht über den internationalen musikwissen-
schaftlichen Kongress, Bonn 1970, p.524-25.
Kassel: Bärenreiter, 1971.
Short paper depicting some historical events in the
development of Japanese musicology, centering around
Beethoven studies.

612. ____. "The Development of Western-Style Music in Japan
and the Position of Japanese Musical Creation." In
Proceedings of the International Round Table on
the Relations between Japanese and Western Arts,
Tokyo and Kyoto, 1968, p.264-73. Tokyo: Japanese
National Commission for UNESCO, 1969.
Reviews the growth of Western music in Japan since
the Meiji Restoration.

613. ____. "Musicology in Japan since 1954." Acta
Musicologica 35(2-3): 47-73, 1963.
Survey of the present situation of musicological
studies in Japan, written primarily for foreigners.
Introduces scholarly societies and institutions for
musicological research, leading instructors and
researchers, and recent noteworthy publications.

614. ____. "Der religiöse Aspekt der japanischen Musik-
geschichte." Musicae Scientiae Collectanea
(Festschrift K.G. Fellerer), p.409-14. Edited by H.
Hüschen. Köln: Arno-Volk Verlag, 1973.
Survey of Japanese music history in religious terms.

615. ____. "Religious Music." In Music--East and West:
Report on 1961 Tokyo East-West Music Encounter
Conference, p.26-29. Tokyo: Executive Committee
for 1961 Tokyo East-West Music Encounter, 1961.
Outline history of religious music in Japan. Argues
for a fusion of the inheritances of Christian and
Buddhist music.

616. NORDGREN, Pehr Henrik. "Neue japanischen Musik." Neue
Zeitschrift für Musik 134(2): 91-94, 1973.
Observations on contemporary Japanese music

(1970's). Points out a characteristic tendency to combine traditional Japanese instruments and modern European composition techniques. Translated from Swedish by Horst Debnar-Daumler.

\* \* \* \* \* \* \* \* \* \* \*

617. OBATA Jûichi, HIROSE Masaji, and TESHIMA Takehiko. "On the Physical Nature of the Characteristic Trill in the Utai, a Japanese Recitative Chant." Proceedings of the Imperial Academy 10(6): 326-29, June 1934.
Results of investigations undertaken by means of an oscillogram into the physical nature of nabiki, a vocal technique used exclusively in nô singing.

618. OBATA Jûichi, OZAWA Yasushirô, and SUGITA Eiji. "Acoustical Investigations of Some Japanese Musical Instruments." Proceedings of the Physico-Mathematical Society of Japan, 3rd S. 12: 285-99; 13: 1-16; 93-105; 133-50, and 190, 1930-31.
Part 1 is devoted to description of the shaku-hachi and examination of the acoustical properties of its sound; Part 2 deals with the shamisen; Part 3 with the tsuzumi; and Part 4 with the koto.

619. OBATA Jûichi and TESHIMA Takehiko. "Further Studies on the Acoustical Properties of the Japanese Wind Instrument, Syakuhati." Proceedings of the Physico-Mathematical Society of Japan, 3rd S. 15: 125-34, 1933.
Deals with the shakuhachi. The directional properties of the sound and the relation between tone-color and blowing pressure are examined.

620. OBATA Toshihiro. The Band in Japan from 1945 to 1970: A Study of Its History and the Factors Influencing Its Growth during This Period. Doctoral dissertation, Michigan State Univ. 1974. 123p.
Discusses the development of band music in Japan from the end of World War II to 1970, and the American influence on its growth.

621. OHTANI Kimiko. The Okinawan Kumiodori: An Analysis of

Relationships of Text, Music and Movement in
Selections from Nidô Tekiuchi. M.A. thesis,
Univ. of Hawaii, 1981. ix, 197p.
Study of a traditional dance-drama created in the
early 18th century in Okinawa. Based on the tran-
scription and analysis of music and body movement of
seven dances performed by the Kin Ryôshô Geinô
Kenkyûjo in 1977.

622. OHTANI Kimiko and TOKUMARU Yoshihiko. "Ethnomusicology
in Japan since 1970." Yearbook for Traditional
Music 15: 155-59, 1983.
Brief outline of ethnomusicological developments in
Japan during the last decade or so. Appends a
selected discography.

623. OKAMOTO N. trans. "Tsubosakadera, oder die wunderbare
Gnade der Göttin Kwannon: Übersetzt von N.
Okamoto; Revidiert und eingeleitet von K. Florenz."
Mittheilungen der Deutschen Gesellschaft für
Natur- und Völkerkunde Ostasiens 9(2): 273-89,
1903.
Translation of Tsubosaka reigenki ("Miracle of
Tsubosaka Temple"), a jôruri play composed by
Toyosawa Danpei II and Kako Chika.

624. OKAZAKI Takeshi. "The Place of Traditional Music in the
Cultivation of Music in Japan." In Challenge in
Music Education, p.374-76. Ed. by F. Callaway.
Nedlands, Western Australia: Univ. of Western
Australia Press, 1976.
Very simple argument for the treatment of Japanese
music in music education in Japan.

625. OKIMOTO, Ray Ichiro. Folk Music of the Dominant Immi-
grant Cultures of Hawaii as Resource for Junior High
School General Music. Doctoral dissertation,
George Peabody College for Teachers, 1974. 171p.
Study includes treatment of the music of Japanese-
Americans in Hawaii.

626. OLSEN, Dale A. "Japanese Music in Brazil." Asian
Music 14(1): 111-31, 1983.
Describes the present state of Japanese music-making
in Brazil, with special focus on the city of Sao
Paulo in 1981.

627. _____. "Japanese Music in Peru." Asian Music 11(2):

41-50, 1980.
Observation of the music-making activities among the
Japanese community in Peru in 1979.

628. _____. "The Social Determinants of Japanese Musical Life
in Peru and Brazil." Ethnomusicology 27(1): 49-
70, 1983.
Comparison of the musical life of Japanese immigrant
populations in two South American countries.
Identifies differences in lifestyle that have an
effect on musical life and styles, and examines the
depth of cultural assimilation of the two
populations.

629. O'NEILL, Patrick G. Early Noh Drama, Its Background,
Character and Development, 1300-1450. London: Lund
Humphries, 1958. 223p.; Reprint ed. Westport, CT:
Greenwood, 1974.
Study of the origins and development of nô. Based
on the author's doctoral dissertation, Sarugaku,
Dengaku and Kusemai in the Creation of Noh Drama,
1300-1450 (Univ. of London, 1957. iv, 451p.).

630. _____. A Guide to Nô. Tokyo & Kyoto: Hinoki
Shoten, 1954. ii, 13, 229p.
General remarks on the nô theater and summa-
ries of 231 plays.

631. _____. "Kyôgen." In Kodansha Encyclopedia of Japan
4: 324-29. Tokyo: Kodansha International, 1983.
Concise survey of the history, schools and players,
play classifications, and other dramatic elements of
kyôgen, including a short section on song,
music and dance.

632. _____. "The Nô Plays Koi no Omoni and Yuya."
Monumenta Nipponica 10: 203-26, 1954.
Translation of the two nô plays with annota-
tions.

633. _____. "The Noh Schools and Their Organization."
Bulletin (Japan Society of London) 4(18): 2-7,
June 1974.
Examination of the methods by which nô performers make their living and organize their stage
performances, with a short historical account and
explanation of the position of the Umewaka family in
relationship to the other five schools.

634. _____. "The Special Kasuga Wakamiya Festival of 1349."
Monumenta Nipponica 14: 408-28, 1958.
Annotated translation of a document, dealing with
the special Wakamiya Festival of 1349, which
provides important evidence concerning the performance of sarugaku and dengaku nô plays
before the influence of Kanze Kan'ami and Zeami.

635. ORTOLANI, Benito. "Das japanische Theater." In
Fernöstliches Theater, p.391-526. Ed. by Heinz
Kindermann. Stuttgart: Kröner, 1966.
Extensive historical survey of Japanese theatrical
forms, dealing with both traditional genres (in
greatest detail with kabuki) and post-Meiji era
modern developments. Includes a bibliography with
both Japanese and European language entries.

636. _____. Das Kabukitheater: Kulturgeschichte der
Anfänge. Tokyo: Sophia Univ. Press, 1964. 169p.
Detailed study of the early history of kabuki,
dealing with its cultural background and sources.
Abbreviated reworking of the author's doctoral
dissertation, Die Anfänge des Kabuki-Theaters.

637. _____. "Okuni-kabuki und Onna-kabuki." Monumenta
Nipponica 17: 161-213, 1962.
Detailed study, based on the author's doctoral
dissertation, of the early history of kabuki
until the banning of onna-kabuki in 1629.
Includes illustrations from the Kunijo kabuki
ekotoba (also known as Okuni kabuki zôshi)
and translation of its text.

638. _____. "Das Wakashû-kabuki und das Yarô-
kabuki." Monumenta Nipponica 18(1-4): 89-127,
1963.
Continuation of the study in Entry 637, dealing with
the early development of kabuki after the banning of onna-kabuki in 1629 through to the
development of yarô-kabuki in the 1650-60's.

639. OSANAI Tadao. "A Research into the Accord of the Shô."
Tôyô Ongaku Kenkyû 16-17: 1-19, 1962.
Attempt to explain the aitake chords of the
shô, a mouthorgan used in the gagaku
ensemble, in terms of the degree of concordance of
each chord.

110

640. ____. "Twice Intermediate Tuning." Tôyô Ongaku
Kenkyû 10-11: 5-21, 1952.
Attempt at producing an evenly-tempered chromatic
scale by means of what the author calls "twice
intermediate tuning," that is, using two intermediate intervals to tune a single interval. Based
on the author's interest in the mathematics of
acoustics.

641. ÔTSUKI Kunio. "Rhythmik und Melodik des älteren
japanischen Kinderlieders." Orff-Institute
Jahrbuch 1963: 80-91. Mainz: B. Schott's Söhne.
Outline of traditional game songs of Japanese
children. Examines their rhythmic and melodic
characteristics.

* * * * * * * * * *

642. PARKER, C.K. and MORISHIMA S. trans. "Kokaji: a Nô
Play in Two Acts." Monumenta Nipponica 3(2):
619-29, 1940.
Translation of Kokaji, with text in both
Japanese and Roman letters.

643. ____. "Shunkan: A Nô Play." Monumenta Nipponica
4(1): 246-55, 1941. NE

644. PENLINGTON, J.N. "Four Drama-Forms of Kabuki."
Transactions of the Asiatic Society of Japan,
2nd S. 1: 83-99, 1924.
Brief historical account of the kabuki theater
and description of its four characteristic drama
forms: sewamono, jidaimono, aragoto and shosa-
goto.

645. PERI, Noël. Cinq Nô. Paris: Bossard, 1921. 259p.
Detailed introduction to the nô play, touching
upon origins of nô, its structure, acting and
dance, costumes and masks. Includes French translation of the following five plays: Oimatsu,
Atsumori, Sotoba-komachi, Ohara-gokô, and Aya
no tsuzumi.

646. ____. Essai sur les gammes japonaises. Paris: Paul

Geuthner, 1934. 70p., bibliog., illus., music.
Discussion of musical scales dealing with gagaku
and zokugaku, and including some folk and
popular songs.

647. _____. Le Nô: Etudes sur le Nô, drame lyrique
japonais. Tokyo: Maison Franco-Japonaise, 1944.
xv, 495p., plates.
Elaborate description and study of the nô
play, followed by French translations of 10 plays,
including in addition to the 5 plays of Entry 645
Miwa, Tamura, Eguchi, Kinuta and Matsuyama-
kagami. Previously published as "Etudes sur le
drame lyrique japonais (Nô)," in Bulletin de
l'Ecole française d'extrême-orient 9(2/4),
11(4), 12(5), 13(4), and 20(1), 1909 20 [Hanoi].

648. PERKINS, P.D. and FUJII Keiichi. "Gosechi-no-mai or Five
Notes Dance." Cultural Nippon 7(3): 97-106,
1939.
Description of the gosechi no mai, an ancient
ritualistic dance performed annually by girls at the
toyonoakari-no-sechie, a Japanese court banquet.

649. _____. "Kagura: A Ceremonial Dance of Japan." Cultural
Nippon 7(1): 37-62, 1939.
Brief history of kagura, the Shintō ritual
song-dance, followed by an examination of the form
and repertoire of present day sato-kagura.

650. _____. "Two Ancient Japanese Dances." Monumenta
Nipponica 3: 314-20, 1940.
Brief description of Matsubayashi ("Music of the
New Year Pines") and Kôwakamai.

651. PHILIPPI, Donald L. trans. Songs of Gods, Songs of
Humans: The Epic Tradition of the Ainu. Foreword
by Gary Snyder. Tokyo: Univ. of Tokyo Press;
Princeton: Princeton Univ. Press, 1978. iv, 417p.,
bibliog.
Extensive introduction to the Ainu and their oral
literature, with translation of 33 representative
selections from the Yukar epics.

652. PICKEN, Laurence E.R. "Central Asian Tunes in the Gagaku
Tradition." In Festschrift Walter Wiora,
p.545-51. Ed. by Ludwig Finscher and Christoph-
Hellmut Mahling. Kassel: Bärenreiter, 1967.

Transcription and analysis of four tunes from the tôgaku repertoire originally linked with Kucha and Ch'ing-hai, countries on the western boundary of the 8th-century T'ang Empire.

653. _____. "Tunes Apt for T'ang Lyrics from the Shô Books of Tôgaku." In Essays in Ethnomusicology: A Birthday Offering for Lee Hye-Kyu, p.401-20. Seoul: Korean Musicological Society, 1969.
Hypothesis that T'ang period tunes have been faithfully preserved in the shô part-books of tôgaku, but that the pace of the original tune has slowed down some 16 times in modern practice.

654. PICKEN, Laurence E.R. and MITANI Yôko. "Finger-techniques for the Zithers sô-no-koto and kin in Heian Times." Musica Asiatica 2: 89-114, 1979.
Attempt to elucidate the meaning of several technical terms used in reference to koto per-formance found in Heian literature, such as the Tale of Genji, by reference to contemporary musical sources.

655. PICKEN, Laurence E.R. and Rembrandt F. WOLPERT. "Mouth-Organ and Lute Parts of Tôgaku and Their Inter-relationships." Musica Asiatica 3: 79-95, 1981.
Transcription and comparison of shô and biwa tablatures from old gagaku part-books, including comparative transcription of ten tô-gaku tunes.

656. PICKEN, Laurence E.R. with Rembrandt WOLPERT, Allan MARETT, Jonathan CONDIT, Elizabeth MARKHAM, and MITANI Yôko. Music from the Tang Court 1. London: Oxford Univ. Press, 1981. 82p., music.
Transcription of the tôgaku suite Ôdai ha-jinraku ("The Emperor Destroys the Military Forma-tions") from manuscripts written between the 8th and 13th centuries. An attempt to recreate the music as it was heard at the T'ang court.

657. PIGGOTT, Francis T. "The Japanese Musical Scale." Transactions and Proceedings of the Japan Society 3: 33-38, 1893.
Concise defence of the author's ideas on the Japanese musical scale as published in earlier works.

658. _____. The Music and Musical Instruments of Japan.
Notes by Thomas L. Southgate. London: B.T. Batsford,
1893. xviiii, 230p.; 2nd ed., 1909. xviii, 196p.,
illus., plates, music; Reprint of the 2nd ed. New
York: Da Capo Press, 1971.
The pioneer work on Japanese music by a Westerner.
As is commonly found in such attempts, there are
numerous misunderstandings and misspelled Japanese
terms. The author's frank reaction and musical
prejudices are of ethnomusicological interest. The
book reveals an obvious lack of perspective, with
heavy emphasis on the genre of koto music.

659. _____. "Music of Japan." Proceedings of the Musical
Association 18: 103-20, 1891-92.
Paper read on April 12, 1892, on the music of Japan,
concentrating on the tuning systems of the koto,
from which conclusions are reached concerning the
nature of the Japanese scale. Information later incorporated into the volume in the previous entry.

660. _____. "The Music of the Japanese." Transactions of
the Asiatic Society of Japan 19: 271-368, 1891.
Paper read on January 14, 1891 on the musical
instruments of Japan. The contents were later
incorporated into the author's book, The Music and
Musical Instruments of Japan. See Entry 658.

661. PIGGOTT, Francis T. and A.H. FOX STRANGWAYS. "Japanese
Music." In Grove's Dictionary of Music and
Musicians, 4th ed. Vol.2, p.764-67. Ed. by H.C.
Colles. London: Macmillan, 1940.
Somewhat unbalanced introduction to Japanese music,
heavily leaning towards koto music. Includes
general remarks on the history of the koto, its
tuning, scales, modes, forms, grace notes, and
harmony.

662. _____, with Laurence PICKEN. "Japanese Music." In
Grove's Dictionary of Music and Musicians, 5th
ed. Vol.4, p.589-93. London: Macmillan, 1954.
Enlarged version of the article in the above entry,
with a few paragraphs under a sub-title "Modern
Music" added by Picken. Introduces works of several
Japanese composers in Western style.

663. POUND, Ezra and Ernest FENOLLOSA. The Classic Noh
Theater of Japan. New York: New Directions, 1959.

163p. First published as 'Noh' or Accomplishment,
a Study of the Classical Stage of Japan. New York:
Knopf, 1917.
Introduction to the nō theater and brief
translations of 14 nō plays, with synopses of
the plots of 4 more plays.

664. PRINGSHEIM, Klaus, "Eine Schicksalfrage des japanischen
Komponisten." Ongaku kenkyū 2: 45-60, 1936.
Argues that it is possible and desirable to express
Japanese thought meaningfully while employing norms
and forms of European music.

665. _____. "Music in Japan." Contemporary Japan 13(2):
231-59, 1944.
Evaluation of the Japanese musician's mastery of
Western music, recommending the eventual
Japanization of music written in Western idioms by
Japanese composers.


* * * * * * * * * * * *


666. RADIO JAPAN, NHK, ed. Twenty Folk Songs of Japan.
Tokyo: Nippon Hōsō Shuppan Kyōkai, 1969. 62p.
Collection of twenty traditional folk songs with
English versions and introductory notes for each
song. Piano accompaniments by D. Guyver Britton.

667. RAZ, Jacob. "The Actor and His Audience: Zeami's Views
on the Audience of the Noh." Monumenta Nipponica
31: 251-74, 1976. NE

668. _____. Audience and Actors: A Study of Their
Interaction in the Japanese Traditional Theatre.
Leiden: E.J. Brill, 1983. 307p.
Historical study of the relationship between actors
and their audience in the Japanese performing arts.
Subjects dealt with include minzoku-geinō,
pre-nō theatrical forms, the nō theater,
kabuki in the Edo period, and modern audiences.

669. READ, Cathleen B. A Study of Yamada-ryū Sōkyoku
and Its Repertoire. Doctoral dissertation,
Wesleyan Univ. 1975. 428p.

Organological examination of the koto and a
brief historical survey of Yamada style
sôkyoku, followed by discussion of its entire
repertoire and analyses of two typical compositions.

670. READ, Cathleen B. and David LOCKE. "An Analysis of the
Yamada-ryu Sokyoku Iemoto System." Hogaku 1(1):
20-52, Spring 1983.
Detailed study of the structure and functions of the
iemoto system of the Yamada school in modern
Japanese society.

671. REID, James L. The Komagaku Repertory of Japanese
Gagaku: A Study of Contemporary Performance
Practice. Doctoral dissertation, UCLA, 1977, 406p.
Stylistic analysis of the komagaku repertory as
practiced today.

672. _____. "Komagaku Works of Japanese Origin." Gagaku
Kai 56: 1 39, 1981.
Examines early sources that ascribe certain koma-
gaku compositions to native Japanese composers.

673. _____. "Transcription in a New Mode." Ethnomusicology 21(3): 415-33, 1977.
Attempt to transcribe Nasori no kyû, a
komagaku composition, in a combination numerical
and graphical notation. See Entry 276 for critical
comments.

674. REINHARD, Kurt. Einführung in die Musikethnologie.
Wolfenbüttel & Zürich: Möseler, 1968. 119p.
Includes a chapter, p.95-111, entitled "Analyse des
altjapanischen Orchesterliedes 'Mushiroda,'" in
which a saibara composition is analyzed in
detail.

675. _____. "Konsonanz und Dissonanz in japanisch Sicht."
Das Musikleben (May 1954): 171-73.
Note on Japanese chords found in music of the
biwa, koto, and shô, and argument that
they are consonant in the Japanese sense though
considered dissonant in the West.

676. REITZ, Karl. "Die Feuerberuhigungszeremonie des Shintô
(Chinkasai)." Monumenta Nipponica 3(1): 109-
26, 1940.
Descriptive introduction to the Hoshizume-

matsuri or Chinka-sai ["Shintô Ritual
Pacifying Fire"], dealing with its history,
philosophy, and ceremonial practice, including
musical aspects such as description of instruments
employed. Facsimiles of Japanese musical notation
are attached.

677. RENONDEAU, Gaston. Nô, Fasc. 1. Tokyo: Maison
Franco-Japonaise, 1953. vii, 205p.
French translation of nô plays with intro-
ductory remarks and notes. Includes the following 6
plays: Funabenkei, Izutsu, Momijigari, Yashima,
Yôrô, and Yoroboshi.

678. _____. Nô, Fasc. 2. Tokyo: Maison Franco-
Japonaise, 1954. 278p., bibliog, list of nô
plays in translation.
French translation of nô plays with
introductory remarks and notes. Includes the
following ten plays: Tsurukame, Kagekiyo, Sagi,
Fujito, Tôru, Maki-ginu, Kiyotsune, Teika, Youchi-
Soga, and Kurama-Tengu.

679. RHODES, Mary R.S. Influence of Japanese Hogaku
Manifest in Selected Compositions by Peter Mennin
and Benjamin Britten. Doctoral dissertation,
Michigan State Univ., 1969. 397p.
Study on the influence of traditional Japanese
music. Examines Mennin's group of four songs (1948)
and Britten's Curlew River (1964) in terms of
the composers' fusion of traditional Japanese music
idiom with their own distinctive styles.

680. RICHIE, Donald. "Japan: 22. Performing Arts." In The
Encyclopedia Americana 15: 783-90. New York:
Americana Corp., 1970.
General survey of Japanese dance, drama, film, and
music, as well as modern dance and ballet in Japan.

681. _____. "Notes on the Noh." Hudson Review 18: 70-80,
Spring 1965.
Rather poetic account of the major features of the
nô drama, with a short section on music which
lacks detail.

682. RICHIE, Donald and WATANABE Miyoko. Six Kabuki
Plays. Tokyo: Hokuseido Press, 1963. 114p.
Translation of the following six plays: Kago-

tsurube, Musume-Dôjôji, Tsubosaka-reigenki, Migawari-zazen, Takatsuki, and Chûshingura.

683. RIMER, Thomas. transl. "Taema: A Noh Play Attributed to Zeami." Monumenta Nipponica 25(4): 431-46, 1970.
Translation, with introduction, of a nô play of the fifth (demon) category.

684. RÖSING, Helmut. "Zur Problematik der Transcription japanischer Palastmusik." Jahrbuch für musikalische Volks- u. Völkerkunde 7: 46-57, 1973.
Discussion of difficulties in transcribing gagaku pieces into Western staff-notation. Argues that transcription of gagaku is meaningless unless combined with sound-recording.

λ λ λ λ λ λ λ λ λ λ λ

685. SADIE, Stanley, ed. "Japan." In New Grove Dictionary of Music and Musicians 9: 504-52. London: Macmillan, 1980.
An extensive entry of 48 pages written by Shigeo Kishibe, D.B. Waterhouse, Robert Garfias, W.P. Malm, Fumio Koizumi, W. Adriaansz, D.P. Berger, Jan LaRue, Kazuyuki Tanimoto, Masataka Kanazawa, and Eishi Kikkawa. The article consists of the following seven sections: I. General, II. Religious Music, III. Theatrical and Courtly Genres, IV. Instruments and Their Music, V. Notation System, VI. Folk Music, VII. Music since 1868. The section of folk music includes Okinawan and Ainu music. See individual authors for annotations.

686. SADLER, Arthur Lindsay, trans. Japanese Plays: Noh, Kyogen, Kabuki. Sydney: Angus and Robertson, 1943. xxvi, 283p.
Translation of 12 nô plays, 24 kyôgen plays, and 4 kabuki plays. Includes short introductory remarks on the histories of the genres.

687. SADLER, A.W. "O-kagura: Field Notes on the Festival Drama in Modern Tokyo." Asian Folklore Studies 29: 275-300, 1970.

Observations on kagura performances at the
Suitengû shrine in Tokyo and at Chichibu, Saitama
Prefecture. Little treatment of music.

688. SAITO, Fred. "Good-by Gagaku, Hello Mozart.: High
Fidelity 18(11): 66-69, November 1968.
Reports on several aspects of contemporary Western
musical activity in Japan. Includes certain statis-
tics.

689. SAKÁNISHI Shio, trans. Japanese Folk-Plays: The
Ink-Smeared Lady and Other Kyogen. Rutland, VT &
Tokyo: Tuttle, 1960. xiii, 150p.
Introduction to kyôgen and translation of 22
plays, with a bibliography of kyôgen litera-
ture and a list of translations.

690. SAKATA, Lorraine. "Comparative Analysis of Sawari on the
Shamisen." Ethnomusicology 10(2): 141-52, 1966.
Investigation of the nature of sawari, a buzzing
sound effect produced on the lowest string of the
shamisen.

691. SAKKA Keisei. "Western Music in Japan." In Music--
East and West: Report on 1961 Tokyo East-West Music
Encounter Conference, p.77-81. Tokyo: Executive
Committee for 1961 TEWMEC, 1961.
Short account of the introduction of Western music
into Japan and the reasons for its rapid growth in
the last century. Postulates an optimistic future
for "Japanese music clothed in Western attire."

692. SAKURAI Chûichi et al, trans. Ze-ami's Kadensho.
Tokyo: Sumiya-Shinobe Publishing Institute, 1968.
109p.
Introduction to and complete translation of the
Kadensho or Fûshi-kaden, Zeami Motokiyo's
treatise on the secrets of the nô play, with
annotations.

693. SANFORD, James H. "Shakuhachi Zen: The Fukeshû
and Komusô." Monumenta Nipponica 32: 411-
40, 1977.
Historical study of the Fuke sect of Zen Buddhism
and the Fuke shakuhachi tradition.

694. SANSOM, Sir George B. "Translations from the No."
Transactions of Asiatic Society of Japan 38(3):

125-65, 1911.
Translation of Funa-benkei and Ataka, two
nô plays by Kanze Nobumitsu.

695. SASAMORI Takefusa. "Impact of Far East Music on American
Music." Hirosaki Daigaku Kyôikugakubu Kiyô
32: 65-81, 1974. [Bulletin of the Faculty of
Education, Hirosaki Univ.]
The section "Japanese Musicians Who Went to America"
contains descriptions of the musical activities of
Japanese immigrants in Hawaii from 1885 to 1930.

696. ____. "The Preservation and Development of the
Performing Arts of Tsugaru." In The Preservation
and Development of the Traditional Performing Arts
[Report of ISCRCP 1980], p.55-61. Tokyo:
Tokyo National Research Institute of Cultural
Properties, 1981.
Discussion of the process of change in the performing arts of the Tsugaru district, Aomori Prefecture, citing examples from Tsugaru-sôkyoku
(koto music), Ajigasaki jinku (a bon dance
song), and Kase no yakko odori (a bon dance).

697. ____. "Shigin: Problem of Transcription and Its Melodic
Form." Hirosaki Daigaku Kyôikugakubu Kiyô
34: 68-80, 1975 [Bulletin of the Faculty of
Education, Hirosaki Univ.]
Preliminary study of shigin, the recitation of
Chinese poems in Japanese pronunciation. Discusses
the problems of its notation and proposes a new
method of transcription.

698. ____. Temari-uta (Japanese Ball-Bouncing Game Song):
An Analysis with Emphasis on Rhythm. M.A.Thesis,
Univ. of Hawaii, 1969. 300p.
Study of the children's game song, analyzing the
structure of song-texts, metric and melodic forms.
Historical accounts of the song-texts are also
provided.

699. SATO Hiroaki and Burton WATSON, eds. and trans. From
the Country of Eight Islands: An Anthology of
Japanese Poetry. Introduction by Thomas Rimer. New
York: Anchor Press, 1981. xliv, 652p.
Sampling of Japanese verses in translation ranging
from the Kojiki to a 19th-century transcript of
a cycle of rice-planting songs. Includes verses from

kagura, saibara, azuma-asobi, fuzoku uta and
from the Ryôjin hishô, as well as the
complete nô play Teika.

700. SATOW, Ernest. "Ancient Japanese Rituals."
Transactions of the Asiatic Society of Japan 7:
95-126(Pt 1), 393-434 (Pt 2), 1879; 9: 183-211 (Pt
3), 1881.
Study of norito, chants used in Shinto rituals, with translations and descriptions of
ceremonies including music. Part 1: Prayer for
Harvest or Toshigoi no matsuri; Part 2: Service
of the God of Kasuga or Kasuga [no] matsuri,
Service and the Goddess of Food or Hirose [no]
oho-imi no matsuri; Part 3: Service of the Temple
of Imaki or Hira nu no matsuri, Luck-Wishing of
the Great Palace or Ohotono hagahi, and Service
of the Gates of the Palace or Mikado matsuri.

701. SCHMID, William R. Introduction to Tribal, Oriental,
and Folk Music. A Rationale and Syllabus for a New
Course for Undergraduate Music Education Curricula
Doctoral dissertation, Eastman School of Music,
1971. 134p.
Includes a little information related to Japanese
music.

702. SCHNEIDER, Ronald. Kôwaka-mai: Sprache und Stil
einer mittelalterlichen japanischen Rezitations-
kunst. Hamburg: Gesellschaft für Natur- und
Völkerkunde Ostasiens, 1968. viii, 305p.
Study of the medieval dance-drama kôwaka-mai,
concerning its origin, creators and bearers,
repertoire, text and literary style. Also deals with
the language of the text in linguistic terms, and
provids translations of two texts: Kosode-goi
and Takadachi. (The author's doctoral dissertation under the same title submitted to Universität
Hamburg, 1967.)

703. SCHÜNEMANN, Georg. "Japanische Musik." Die Musik
33(1): 237-40, October 1940.
General remarks on Japanese music. Introduces
aspects of the nô play, gagaku and of the
koto and shamisen music.

704. _____. "Japanische Schulmusik." Musikpflege 3: 373-
82, 1932-33.

Short description of the place of European music in
Japanese music education in the 1930's, with an
introduction to a number of songs sung at elementary
school level. The positive reactions of the author
may reflect the atmosphere of the pre-War decade.

705. _____. "Musik in Japan." In Kulturmacht Japan, p.63-
66. Vienna: Die Pause, 1942.
Brief introduction to Japanese music, with
illustrations.

706. SCHWARTZ, W. L. "The Great Shrine of Idzumo: Some Notes
on Shintô, Ancient and Modern." Transactions of
the Asiatic Society of Japan 41: 493-681. 1913.
Chapter 3 "The Daily Routine and Festivals of the
Great Shrine" contains descriptions of music and
musical instruments used in Shintô rituals.

707. SCOTT, Adolph C. Genyadana: A Japanese Kabuki Play.
Tokyo: Hokuocido Preoo, 1953. 52p., illuo.
Introduction and synopsis of Gen'yadana, a
famous scene from the play Yo wa nasake ukina no
yokoguohi written by Sogawa Jokô III (1806-81),
followed by a translation of the play.

708. _____. The Kabuki Theatre of Japan. London: Allen
and Unwin, 1955.
General discussion of kabuki in all its aspects,
including music and dance, with summaries of six
plays.

709. _____. Kanjinchô: A Japanese Kabuki Play. Tokyo:
Hokuseido Press, 1953. 50p.
Short study of Kanjinchô, which includes an
introduction, plot summary and translation of the
play.

710. _____. The Puppet Theatre of Japan. Rutland, VT &
Tokyo: Tuttle, 1963. 163., illus.
Historical outline of the Japanese puppet theater
bunraku, with description of ten famous plays.

711. _____. "Reflections on the Aesthetic Background of the
Performing Arts of East Asia." Asian Music 6 (1-
2): 207-16, 1975. [Perspectives on Asian Music:
Essays in Honor of Dr. Laurence E. R. Picken]
Article dealing with the influence of Zen Buddhism
on the underlying aesthetic of performing arts in

122

East Asia. Little treatment of specific examples and
no actual treatment of music.

712. _____. "Theater, Traditional." In Kodansha
Encyclopedia of Japan 8: 21-23. Tokyo: Kodansha
International, 1983.
Survey of five major genres of Japanese traditional
theater (bugaku, nô, kyôgen, bunraku, and
kabuki) that attempts to view them in terms of
Asian drama as a whole, and which compares
kabuki with China's Peking opera.

713. SEIDENSTICKER, Edward. Low City, High City: Tokyo from
Edo to the Earthquake. New York: Alfred A. Knopf,
1983. ix, 302p., maps, photos.
Includes a vivid description of the musical and theatrical life of Tokyo from the mid-nineteenth century to 1923, dealing with such things as the kabuki theater and nô theaters, music halls,
opera, yose, Yoshiwara festivals, etc.

714. _____. transl. The Tale of Genji. 2 vols. New York:
Alfred A. Knopf, 1977. 1090p.
Murasaki Shikibu's novel depicting 10th-century
Heian court life. There are numerous musical
references, which are in general faithfully
translated.

715. SESAR, Carl. "China vs. Japan: The Noh Play Haku
Rakuten." In Chinese and Japanese Music-Drama,
p.143-69. Ed. by J. I. Crump and W. P. Malm. Ann
Arbor: Center for Chinese Studies, Univ. of
Michigan, 1975.
Remarks on certain types of nô plays in which
the question of Japan's cultural relationship to
China is treated as the central theme, with analysis
of the nô play Haku Rakuten, as a music-
drama.

716. SETOGUCHI Tokichi. "Military Music in Japan."
Contemporary Japan 1: 532-34, 1932-33.
Brief historical account of Japanese military music.
An abridged version of an article written in
Japanese and published earlier in the Bungei
Shunjû, October 1932.

717. SHIBA Sukehiro. Gagaku 2 vols. Tokyo: Ryûgin-Sha,
1955-56.

Scores of Japanese court music in Western notation.
Vol.1 is a collection of six kangen (orchestral)
pieces. Vol.2 is a collection of six saibara
(vocal) compositions. Accompanied by brief
commentaries in Japanese, English, and French.

718. ____. "The Music of Japan (Gagaku)." In Music--East
and West: Report of 1961 Tokyo East-West Music
Encounter Conference, p.9-11. Tokyo: Executive
Committee for 1961 TEWMEC, 1961.
General remarks on the tradition of gagaku and
its performers.

719. ____. "The Tones of Ancient Oriental Music and Those of
Western Music." KBS Bulletin 13: 6-8, July 1955.
Brief historical survey of the Sino Japanese tone
system.

720. SHIBANO, Dorothy T. "Suehirogari. The Fan of
Felicity." Monumenta Nipponica 35: 77-88, 1980.
Introduction to and translation of a waki-
kyôgen or auspicious comic drama performed at
the nô theater.

721. SHIBATA Minao. "Music and Technology in Japan." In
Music and Technology, p.173-79. Ed. by W.
Skyvington. Paris: Richard-Masse, 1971. [La Revue
musicale Nos. 239-40]
Paper presented at the Stockholm meeting "Music and
Technology," held June 8-12, 1970. Brief historical
account of activities of outstanding Japanese
composers in the 1950's and '60's, focusing on the
use of electrophonic media.

722. SHIDEHARA Michitarô and Wilfred WHITEHOUSE, transl.
"Seami Jûroku Bushû: Seami's Sixteen Treatises."
Monumenta Nipponica 4(2): 530-65, 1941; 5(2)
466-500, 1942.
Partial translation of Zeami Motokiyo's Fûshi-
kaden ("The Flower in Form."). The introduction
and chapters 1, 2, 3 (Nenrai keiko jôjô,
Monomane jôjô, Mondô jôjô) and chapter 4
(Jingi ni iu) are included.

723. SHIMAZAKI Chifumi. The Noh, Vol.1: God Noh. Tokyo:
Hinoki shoten, 1972. xviii, 322p.
Translations of the plays Takasago, Oimatsu,
Yôrô, Kamo, Ema, and Seiôbo, with a

general introduction and commentary.

724. SHINOHARA Makoto. "Neue Musik in Japan." Neue
Zeitschrift für Musik 4: 340–47, 1981.
A survey of contemporary Japanese music, focusing on
approaches and trends in new music of Western style.

725. SHIVELY Donald H. "Bakufu versus Kabuki," Harvard
Journal of Asiatic Studies 18: 326–56, 1955.
Outline of a series of oppressive measures enacted
by the Tokugawa government against kabuki,
including the successive banning of onna kabuki
(women's kabuki) and wakashû kabuki (youth's
kabuki), and the licencing of yarô kabuki
(fellow's kabuki). Little treatment of musical
matters.

726. SHUMWAY, Larry V. Kibigaku: An Analysis of a Modern
Japanese Ritual Music. Doctoral dissertation,
Univ. of Washington, 1974. 291p.
Study of a musical tradition which was created in
1872 by Kishimoto Yoshihide of Okayama, a gagaku
musician. General remarks on the tradition and
stylistic analysis.

727. SIEBOLD, Philipp Franz von [collected by]. Japanische
Melodien. Wien, 1874. 6p. Arranged for the klavier
[by J. Küffner].
Reprint of the 1836 Leiden edition. Contains a
popular song Anoko mitasani.

728. _____. Nippon: Archiv zur Beschreibung von Japan.
[Leiden: by the author, 1832]. Second ed. Würzburg &
Leipzig: Verlag der K.U.K. Hofbuchhandlung von Leo
Woerl, 1897.
Section on Japanese religions describes aspects of
Japanese rituals; sections on Ryûkyû Islands,
the Ainu lands and Sakhalin record some information
concerning song, dance and musical instruments.
Plates illustrate many musical instruments and
dances.

729. SIEFFERT, René. "The Literary Sources of the Noh."
World of Music 17(3): 13–18, 1975.
The texts of various nô plays are viewed in
terms of their libretti, and compared with their
literary sources.

730. _____. "The Literary Sources of the Noh." World of
     Music 25(1): 44-54, 1983.
     Account of the major literary sources used by
     authors of nô plays, pointing out the great
     importance of epic poems such as Heike
     monogatari. Argues that the difficulties
     encountered in the modern understanding of nô
     generally result from modern ignorance of these
     literary sources.

731. _____. "Mibu-kyôgen." Bulletin de la Maison
     Franco-Japonaise n.s.3: 117-51, 1953.
     Description of Mibu-kyôgen, a medieval ritual
     dance-drama handed down at the Mibu temple of Kyoto;
     its history and repertoire.

732. _____. "Le Théâtre japonais." In Grande Encyclo-
     pédie, p.6654-58. Paris: Librairie Larousse, 1974.
     Brief survey of the Japanese theatrical arts, intro-
     ducing gigaku, bugaku, nô, ningyô-jôruri,
     kabuki, and contemporary theater.

733. SIGNELL, Karl. "The Modernization Process in Two
     Occidental Music Cultures: Turkish and Japanese."
     Asian Music 7(2): 72-102, 1976.
     Discussion of "modernization" and "Europeanization"
     in music, citing examples from Turkey and Japan.

734. SISAURI, V. "Yaponskaya muzyka gagaku." Sovetskaya
     muzyka 1: 129-34, 1975. (in Russian)
     General remarks on Japanese court music for Russian
     readers.

735. _____. Protsess formirovaniia i geneticheskie sviazi
     iaponskoi instrumental'noi muzyki gagaku. Doctoral
     dissertation, Leningradskii gosudartvennyi institut
     teatra, muzyki i kinematografii, 1975. (in Russian)
     "The Formative Process and Genetic Links of the
     Japanese Instrumental Music of Gagaku." NE

736. SLEEPER, William W. ed. Native Melodies: For Use in
     Missionary Meetings and Expositions-- Japanese.
     New York: The Young People's Missionary Movement,
     1911. 8p.
     Collection of eight Japanese songs with translations
     of the song-texts.

737. SMITH, Barbara. "The Bon-Odori in Hawaii and Japan."

Journal of International Folk Music Council 14:
36-39, 1962.
Discussion of the bon festival music and dance
brought into Hawaii by Japanese immigrants and its
later variations.

738. SMITH, Laura A. "The Music of Japan." The Nineteenth
Century 36: 900-18, July-Decemeber 1894.
Essay introducing Japanese music to Westerners,
quoting a number of folk and popular songs. Includes
music and translations of the texts.

739. STANGLEIGH, H. Jones, Jr. trans. "The Nô Plays
Obasute and Kanehira." Monumenta Nipponica 18(1-4): 261-85, 1963.
Translations, with short introduction, of two
nô plays attributed to Zeami Motokiyo.

740. SUGINO Masayoshi. "Die Anfänge des japanischen Theaters
bis zum Nôspiel." Monumenta Nipponica 3: 90-
108, 1940.
Outline history of performing arts in Japan from the
earliest historical sources until the period of
nô play.

741. SUGIYAMA Makoto and FUJIMA Kanjûrô. An Outline
of the Japanese Dance. Tokyo: Kokusai Bunka
Shinkokai, 1937. 33p.
Brief historical introduction to the Japanese
classical dance genres kagura, gigaku, bugaku,
nô, and kabuki dance. Illustrations include
demonstrations of dance positions by Fujima
Kanjûrô.

742. SUNAGA Katsumi. Japanese Music. Tokyo: Board of
Tourist Industry, Japanese Government Railways,
1936. 66p., illus. [Tourist Library 15]
Brief introduction to the music and musical
instruments of Japan, primarily for foreign
tourists.

743. SUPPAN, Wolfgang and SAKANISHI Hachiro. "Musikforschung
in und für Japan." Acta Musicologica 54(1-2):
84-123, 1982.
General outline of musicology in and on Japan for
six to seven years preceding 1982, with bibliography. Divided broadly into two sections (non-
Japanese and Japanese music); the section on

Japanese music is further subdivided into subsections dealing with specific genres, instruments,
etc. Bibliography includes works in both Japanese
and European languages.

744. SUTTON, R. Anderson. "Okinawan Music Overseas: A
Hawaiian Home." Asian Music 15(1): 54-80, 1983.
Sociological study of Okinawan music in Hawaii,
dealing with the history of Okinawan immigration to
Hawaii, a description of their music culture in
contemporary terms, and hypothesis of reasons for
the unique configuration of that music culture.

745. SYLE, Revd. Dr. "On Primitive Music, Especially That of
Japan." Transactions of the Asiatic Society of
Japan 5(1): 170-79, 1877.
One of the early curious approaches to Japanese
music. Includes a comparison of the size of
intervals used on the koto with the Pythagorian
scale and the "natural gamut with flats and sharps."


\* \* \* \* \* \* \* \* \* \* \*


746. TAJIMA Mami. "The Fate of Nagoya's Mechanical Festival
Floats." Asian Folklore Studies 42(2): 181-208,
1982.
Detailed description of the Fukurokuju float of the
Wakamiya Hachiman Festival of Nagoya, which uses
karakuri ningyô or mechanical puppets. The
author treats music and musicians as one of the
three essential elements of the performance on the
float, and makes interesting observations in regard
to the method of transmission of the music.

747. TAKAMI Tomiko. "Methods of Learning Folk Music and Their
Influence on the Music Itself: The Case of Etchû
Owara-bushi." In Preservation and Development
of the Traditional Performing Arts [Report of
ISCRCP 1980] p.12-27. Tokyo: Tokyo National Research
Institute of Cultural Properties, 1981.
Examination of changes brought about in a bon
dance song of Toyama Prefecture by the process of
transmission.

128

748. _____. "The Sonic Organization of Fushiuta from the
      Yaeyama Islands." In Musical Voices of Asia
      [Report of ATPA 1978], p.125–30. Tokyo: Japan
      Foundation, 1980.
      Study of a folk song genre of an island group in
      Okinawa. Deals with the functions of each of its
      accompanying instruments.

749. TAKANO Kiyoshi. "Theorie der japanischen Musik 1: Unter-
      suchungen über die Form der 'Koto'-Musik 'Dammono'."
      Tôhoku Psychologica Folia 3: 69–169, 1935.
      Somewhat laborious study of the danmono form of
      sôkyoku or koto music. Outline history of
      koto music is followed by a discussion of the
      danmono genre and its form. Concludes that the
      danmono form resembles the European sonata form.
      Transcription of eight danmono pieces given as
      appendix.

750. _____. "Theorie der japanischen Music 2: Untersuchungen
      über das instrumentale Zwischenspiel in Anfang der
      'Ziuta'-Form." Tôhoku Psychologica Folia 4:
      93–130, 1936.
      Study of the tegoto of jiuta, with general
      remarks on the culture and music of 17th- and
      18th-century Japan, the origin of shamisen music
      and analysis of eight jiuta compositions.

751. TAKANO Kiyosi and INADA Taiiti. "Über das Falschsingen
      beim japanischen Kinderlied." Tôhoku Psycho-
      logica Folia 6(4): 189–201, 1938.
      Study of the idiosyncracies of variant versions of
      school and folksongs sung by Japanese children.

752. TAKAYA, Ted Terujiro. An Inquiry into the Role of the
      Traditional Kabuki Playwright. Doctoral disser-
      tation, Columbia Univ., 1969. v, 202p. NE

753. _____. "Kabuki." In Kodansha Encyclopedia of Japan
      14: 90–97, 1983. Tokyo: Kodansha International,
      1983.
      Survey of the kabuki theater-form, dealing with
      its history, music, dance, types of kabuki plays
      and its dramatic characteristics.

754. TAKEDA Akimichi. "The Education of Professional
      Musicians and their Public in Traditional Western
      Music in Japan." International Music Education:

129

ISME Yearbook 2: 17-20, 1974.
Outlines the situation of music education in Western
music in Japan and advocates the development of
"creativity" on the part of performers and listeners
alike as a means of assimilation.

755. _____. "Japan: Shomyo or Schubert." World of Music
14(4): 48-57, 1972.
Critical essay on the heavily Western-oriented state
of music and music education in Japan today, calling
for attention to the condition of Japan's own music.

756. _____. "Musikleben und Musikerziehung in Japan." Das
Orchester 21(2): 731-33, 1973.
Discussion of the problem of Japanese music education in terms of the conflict between imported classical Western music and traditional Japanese music.

757. TAMBA Akira. "Aesthetics in the Traditional Music of
Japan." World of Music 18(2): 3-10, 1976.
Attempts to shed light on the principal aspects of
the aesthetics that govern the organization of traditional Japanese music.

758. _____. "Aspect religieux de la musique du Nô." In
Encyclopédie des musiques sacrées 1: 214-21. Ed.
by Jaques Porte. Paris: Editions Labergerie, 1968.
Brief analytical introduction to the music of the
nô theater.

759. _____. "La Comparaison de la notion de terms dans la
musique japonaise et dans la musique occidentale."
In Le Japon vu depuis la France: Les études
japonaise en France, p.77-85. Tokyo: La Maison
Franco-Japonaise, 1981.
Attempts to explain the specific character of
musical expression in Japan by comparing two strik-
ingly different notions of time in Japan and the
West. Cites the nine degrees of rhythm in the
nô play.

760. _____. "Confluence of Spiritual and Aesthetic Research
in Traditional Japanese Music." World of Music
25(1): 30-43, 1983.
Attempt at outlining the relationships existing between traditional Japanese music and Buddhist philosophy, centering on nô drama and its music.

130

761. ____. "The Music of the Noh." World of Music 17
(3): 3-12, 1975.
General remarks on the music of the nô theater, touching upon its history, structure, the
principle of jo-ha-kyû, rhythmic characteristics, instruments and kakegoe (vocal interjections). Followed by a selected discography.

762. ____. "Signification des cris dans la musique du Nö."
Revues d'esthétique 24(2): 160-66, 1971.
Examines two functions of the drummers' calls
(kakegoe) in the nô play. The stylized
voices of the drummers had originally nothing but
musical significance, but a spiritual aspect was
later incorporated under the influence of Zen
Buddhism.

763. ____. La Structure musicale du Nô, théatre
traditionnel japonais. Paris: Klincksieck, 1974.
254p., illus., bibliog., discog., two 7-inch discs.
Study devoted to musical aspects of the nô
theater. Consists of introductory remarks on the
definition of nô, a historical outline, and
sections dealing with the repertory and its
categories, the structure of a play, performers, and
aspects of the vocal and instrumental music. Based
on La Musique de Nô, théâtre traditionnel
japonais, Doctoral dissertaion, Univ. de Paris IV,
1971. 223p. Subsequent English version published as
The Musical Structure of Nô. Translated by
Patricia Matoré. Tokyo: Tokai Univ. Press, 1981.
242p.

764. ____. "Symbolic Meaning of Cries in the Music of Noh."
World of Music 20(3): 107-19, 1978.
Inquiry into kakegoe, or vocal interjections, of
the nô theater. Describes the possible relationship between the musical technique of nô
and the convergence of an aesthetic spirituality.

765. ____. "The Use of Masks in the Nô Theatre." World
of Music 22(1): 39-52, 1980.
On the history of masked dance-drama in Japan.
Includes discussion of the manner in which masks are
used in the nô theater, and the acoustical
properties of the nô mask. With a brief German
summary.

766. TAMBA Akira and Michèle CASTELLEGNO. "La Musique du
     théâtre nô japonais." Bulletin du Groupe
     d'acoustique musicale 39: 1-29, 1969. Examination
     of the constituent elements of nô, the vocal
     and instrumental parts, and a study of its
     instruments, with acoustical analyses.

767. TANABE Hideo. "Some Remarks on the Present State of
     Japanese Traditional Music." In Proceedings of the
     Second Asian Pacific Music Conference, p.23-25.
     1977.
     Brief note on the characteristics of traditional
     music and recent trends towards its introduction
     into music curricula at compulsory education level.

768. _____. "Western Influences on Japanese Music." In the
     Proceedings of the First Asian Pacific Music Con-
     ference (October 12-18, 1975), 35-40p. Seoul:
     Cultural and Social Centre for the Asian and Pacific
     Region, 1975. Republished in Asia and Pacific
     Quarterly of Cultural and Social Affairs 7(4):
     17-22, Spring 1976.
     General remarks concerning Japanese music, both
     traditional and Western-style, since the Meiji
     Restoration, referring particularly to European
     influences on traditional music and musicians, and
     to modern compositions.

769. TANABE Hisao. "Japanese Music." The Asian Review 2
     (5): 498-501, July-August 1921.
     Briefly traces the history of Japanese music in
     terms of three stages of development: 1) the period
     from the unrecorded past to the 5th-century; 2)
     5th-century to early 13th-century; 3) 13th-century
     to the present.

770. _____. Japanese Music. 2nd ed. Tokyo: Kokusai Bunka
     Shinkokai, 1959. 74p. illus., music. Revised version
     of the 1st ed. (1929).
     Outline of Japanese music, both traditional and
     Western, written for foreigners. Contains eight
     traditional pieces transcribed into five-line staff
     notation.

771. _____. "Japanese Musical Instruments." In The Japanese
     Music, p.39-115. Tokyo: Japanese National
     Committee of the International Music Council, 1967.
     Introductory discourse concerning major genres of

traditional Japanese music and musical scales,
followed by an extensive description of
representative instruments including the koto,
kin, biwa, shamisen, kokyû, fue, shakuhachi,
hichiriki, shô, taiko, kakko, tsuzumi, etc.

772. ____. "Music in Japan." In Western Influences in
Modern Japan, p.469-523. Ed. by Nitobe Inazo.
Chicago: Univ. of Chicago Press, 1931.
Attempt to describe the origin, to trace the
historical development, and to estimate the value of
music in Japan. Consists of two parts: Pt.1 is devoted to traditional music styles, and Pt.2 deals
with Western music in Japan after the Meiji Restoration.

773. ____. "Recent Researches in Japanese Musical Instruments." The Japan Magazine 16(6): 181-86,
March-April 1926.
Inquiry into the origin of the shamisen,
introducing a few historical sources. The author
reveals his far-reaching hypothesis that the
shamisen may be related to the ancient
nabla.

774. TANAKA Hideo. "A Research in Degree of Affinity among
Entertainment Programmes." Tôhoku Psychologica
Folia 8(2): 83-98, 1940.
Report on 1938 study of listeners' preferences in
relation to entertainment programs, including
various styles of traditional Japanese music as well
as popular and classical Western music.

775. TANIMOTO Kazuyuki. "Ainu Music." [Part of §VI. Folk
Music, sub-entry of the article "Japan"]. In New
Grove Dictionary of Music and Musicians 9: 548-49.
London: Macmillan, 1980.
Brief survey of the music of the Ainu people.

776. ____. "Music of the Ainu." In Proceedings of the
Centennial Workshop on Ethnomusicology Held at the
University of British Columbia, Vancouver, June
19 to 23, 1967, p.60-67. Ed. by Peter Crossley-
Holland. Vancouver: Government of the Province of
British Columbia, 1968.
General remarks on the present condition of tradi-
tional Ainu music.

777. _____. "The Present Condition of the Preservation and
Study of Ainu Music." In Preservation and Devel-
opment of Traditional Performing Arts [Report of
ISCRCP 1980], p.129-33. Tokyo: Tokyo National
Research Institute of Cultural Properties, 1981.
Report on Ainu music documentation and studies.

778. TEELE, Roy E. "The Structure of the Japanese Noh Play."
Chinese and Japanese Music-Dramas, p.189-214.
Ed. by J.I. Crump and W.P. Malm. Ann Arbor, MI:
Center for Chinese Studies, Univ. of Michigan, 1975.
Conference paper dealing with the relationship
between traditional theoretical guidelines for
analysis of nô plays and the actual structure
of a large number of plays.

779. _____. "Translations of Noh Plays." Comparative
Literature 9: 345-68. 1957.
Comparative guide to translations of nô plays
into European languages made before 1956, with
extensive bibliography and list of plays translated.

780. TERADA Torahiko. "Acoustical Investigation of the
Japanese Bamboo Pipe Syakuhati." The Journal of
the College of Science, Imperial University of
Tôkyô 21(10): 1-34, 1907.
General remarks on the shakuhachi with an examination of the special functions of the mouth in producing different varieties of tone, and a study of
the effects of the lateral openings (finger-holes)
of the instrument in general.

781. _____. "Note on Vibrations of Drum." In Proceedings of
the Tôkyô Mathematico-Physical Society 4: 345-
50, 1908.
Study concerning the mode of vibration of the
membrane stretched on one end of a cylinder and that
of the air column within it.

782. _____. "On Syakuhati." Proceedings of the Tôkyô
Mathematico-Physical Society 3: 83-87, 1906.
An attempt to elucidate the characteristic features
of aerial vibration in an end-blown flute like the
shakuhachi.

783. TERASAKI Etsuko T. A Study of Genzai Plays in the Noh
Drama. Doctoral dissertation, Columbia Univ.,
1969. 227p.

134

Deals with the genzai category of nô, its
authors, and the concept of reality revealed in the
plays.

784. THOMPSON, Robin. "Gagaku and European Contemporary
Music: Thoughts Occasioned by the Première of
Stockhausen's 'Hikari'." Gagaku Kai 54: 1-9,
1978,
Critical comment on Stockhausen's composition
Licht-Hikari-Light: Der Jahrslauf for four court
dancers and gagaku orchestra, 1977.

785. _____. "A Study of the Gagaku Composition 'Ringa'."
Gagaku Kai 55: 1-19, 1980.
Analytical study of Ringa, a piece in the
komagaku repertoire of gagaku.

786. TODA Kunio. "Notes sur la musique de Nô." In La
Musique et ses problèmes contemporains (Cahiers de
la compagnie Madleine Renard—Jean-Louis Barrault)
1953-1963, p.331-54. Paris: Edition René Julliard,
1963.
General remarks on music of the nô theater,
dealing with rhythm, musical scales, tonality and
polyphony, form and other features.

787. TÔGI Masatarô. "Bugaku: Ancient Japanese Music and
Dance." In Bugaku, p.21-32. Ed. by Umeda
Ryôzô. Tokyo: Ôtsuka Kôgeisha, 1973.
Outlines the history of bugaku and gagaku,
Japanese court dance and orchestra. Commentary
accompanies a color photo album of bugaku (84
plates).

788. _____. Gagaku: Court Music and Dance. Translated by
Don Kenny, with an introduction by William P. Malm.
New York & Tokyo: Walker/Weatherhill, 1971. 207p.
220 plates and a chronology.
Introduction to gagaku and bugaku by a renowned court musician and dancer, with numerous
illustrations.

789. TOITA Yasuji. Kabuki: The Popular Theater.
Translated by Don Kenny. Introduction by Donald
Keene. New York, Tokyo & Kyoto: Weatherhill/
Tankosha, 1970. viii, 245p.
Originally published in Japanese under the title
Kabuki (Tankosha, Kyoto).

790. TOKI Zenmaro. Japanese Nô Plays. Tokyo: Japan
Travel Bureau, 1954. 204p., illus., bibliog.
Introductory study of nô written as one of a
series designed to give tourists basic knowledge of
various phases of Japanese culture. Copiously illustrated.

791. TOKUMARU Yoshihiko. L'Aspect mélodique de la musique
de syamisen. Doctoral dissertation, École de
Musique, Université Laval, 1981. viii, 222p.
Study of the shamisen and its music. Presents a
new theory concerning the tonal system found in
shamisen music.

792. _____. "Le mouvement mélodique et le système tonal de
la musique de syamisen." Canadian University Music
Review 1: 66–105, 1980.
Re-examination of the tonal system and modal characteristics of music genres accompanied by the
shamisen.

793. _____. "Some Remarks on the Shamisen and Its Music." In
Asian Musics in an Asian Perspective [Report of
ATPA], p.90–99. Tokyo: Japan Foundation, 1977.
Study of the shamisen in terms of its construc-
tion and music. Deals with differences among the
various types of shamisen of the present-day.

794. _____. 'Volksmusik.' Part of article "Musik." In
Japan-Handbuch, col.1284–94. Ed. by H.
Hammitzsch. Wiesbaden: Franz Steiner, 1981.
Outline of the major genres of Japanese folk performing arts, with treatment of their major musical
features. Also deals with modern entertainment
music.

795. TOKYO ACADEMY OF MUSIC, comp. Brief Description of
the Tokyo Academy of Music. Tokyo, 1931. 8p.
Includes details of the establishment of a course
in Japanese music, with the sections nagauta,
nôgaku, sôkyoku, and nôgaku-hayashi.

796. _____, comp. Collection of Japanese Koto Music
[Sôkyoku Shû]. Tokyo: [Monbushô] 1888. ii,
37p. (music); ii (preface in Japanese), 12p. (Song-
texts in Japanese).
One of the earliest published collections of five-
line staff notation containing 15 pieces of koto

music, compiled by members of the Music Study Committee, supervised by Isawa Shûji, director. The
English preface is dated September 1, 1888. The
song-texts are romanized in the notation; no translation is provided.

797. TOKYO NATIONAL RESEARCH INSTITUTE OF CULTURAL PROPER-
TIES, ed. Preservation and Development of the
Traditional Performing Arts [Report of the Fourth
International Symposium on the Conservation and Restoration of Cultural Property, August 6-9, 1980].
Tokyo: Organizing Committee of ISCRCP, Tokyo National Research Institute of Cultural Properties, 1981.
Includes 14 papers concerning Japanese music,
musical instruments, and music education centering
around the subject of preservation and development
in the performing arts.

798. TÔYAMA Kazuyuki. "La musique au Japon." In La grande
encyclopédie, p.6663. Paris: Librairie Larousse,
1974.
Cursory historical survey of Japanese music.

799. TRAN Van Khê. "Problem of Sino-Japanese Music Tradition Today." In Music--East amd West: Report on
1961 Tokyo East-West Music Encounter Conference,
p.54-59.
Proposals for the preservation, revitalization, and
international cultural exchange of the traditional
musics of East Asia.

800. _____. "Le Théâtre musical en Chine, au Japon et au
Viet-Nam." Bulletins 14/15: 1-13, 1974-75.
Paris: Centre d'Etudes de Musique orientale, Univ.
de Paris-Sorbonne.
Comparison of the theatrical arts among three
cultures in East Asia.

801. TRAYNOR, Leo and KISHIBE Shigeo. "The Four Unknown Pipes
of the Shô." Tôyô Ongaku Kenkyû 9: 26-
53, 1951.
Investigation concerning the four pipes no longer
voiced on the modern Japanese shô (mouth-
organ). Making reference to ancient musical treatises, the authors suggest that the pipes were once
actually used, and advance probable tunings for each
pipe.

802. TRUMBULL, Suzanne. "Introduction to Kabuki." _Japan_
     _Magazine_ 1: 28-31, Summer 1957. NE

803. TSUBOUCHI Shôyô and YAMAMOTO Jirô. _History_ and
     _Characteristics_ of _Kabuki, the Japanese Classical_
     _Drama._ Translated by Ryôzô Matsumoto.
     Yokohama: Yamagata, 1960. 319p.
     English translation of _Kabuki no rekishi to sono_
     _tokushitsu._

804. TSUDA Michiko. "Jiuta Shamisen Tunings: A Study of Its
     History and Development." _Tôyô Ongaku Ken-_
     _kyû_ 34-37: 84-125, 1974.
     Discussion of the tuning systems of the _shamisen_
     employed in the genre _jiuta._ Historical consid-
     eration is presented by means of examination of the
     types of tuning changes made by the performer in the
     course of playing a single composition.

805. TSUDZUMI Tsuneyoshi. _Die Kunst Japans._ Leipzig:
     Insel-Verlag, 1929. 341p., illus., music.
     Section "Musik" (p.300-26) is an introductory study
     of the music of Japan, outlining in somewhat
     romantic terms the Japanese attitude towards sound,
     and giving a broad historical picture of the
     development of Japanese music. Appends 8 transcrip-
     tions.

806. TSUGAWA Shuichi. "The Christian Influence upon Music in
     Japan." _The Japan Mission Year Book_ (1929):
     225-32.
     Somewhat biased view of the influence of Protestant
     Christianity on music in Japan in the 60 years prior
     to 1929.

807. TSUGE Gen'ichi. "Another Way of Preserving and Develop-
     ing the Traditional Performing Arts." In _Pres-_
     _ervation and Development of the Traditional Perform-_
     _ing Arts_ [Report of ISCRCP 1980], p.149-53. Tokyo:
     Tokyo National Institute of Cultural Properties,
     1981.
     Proposal for more active international cultural
     exchanges and research through the mutual study of
     performing arts.

808. _____, comp. and transl. _Anthology of Sôkyoku and_
     _Jiuta Song Texts._ Foreword by David P. McAllester.
     Tokyo: Academia Music, 1983. xvi, 220p.

Translation of the texts of 90 pieces from the
jiuta-sôkyoku repertoire, including 32 koto-
kumiuta, 23 jiuta pieces, and 18 compositions
of the Yamada-style sôkyoku repertoire. With
the original song texts in both Japanese and
romanized versions.

809. _____. "Bamboo, Silk, Dragon and Phoenix: Symbolism in
the Musical Instruments of Asia." World of Music
20(3): 10-23, 1978.
Discussion of some symbolic aspects of certain
Japanese and other Asian instruments, in terms of
materials, shape, and nomenclature.

810. _____. "The History of the Kyotaku." Asian Music
8(2): 47-63, 1977.
Introduction to and translation of the Kyotaku
denki kokujikai, a legendary history of the
kyotaku, or fuke-shakuhachi, and its
tradition.

811. _____. "Japans traditionelle Musik: Einige persönliche
Wahrnehmungen." Neue Zeitschrift für Musik 4:
334-39, July-August 1981.
Some personal observations on certain unique aspects
of traditional Japanese music, including elements of
performance, instruments, and notation.

812. _____. "Musical Idols: Beasts in the Form of
Instruments." Articles on Asian Music: Festschrift
for Dr. Chang Sa-hun, p.407-19. Seoul: Korean
Musicological Society, 1977.
Examination of zoömorphic aspects of Asian instru-
ments, including some Japanese musical instruments.

813. _____. "Raiment of Traditional Japanese Musicians--Its
Social and Musical Significance." World of Music
25(1): 55-69, 1983.
Explanation of the social and musical implications
of clothing worn by musicians in a number of genres
of Japanese music.

814. _____."Symbolic Techniques in Japanese Koto-Kumiuta."
Asian Music 12(2): 109-32, 1981.
Discussion of a particular attitude of Japanese
toward "sound," and an examination of certain types
of instrumental techniques that symbolize sounds of
nature and reflect this particular attitude, as

employed in koto kumiuta.

815. TSUJI Shôichi. "The Tale of Genji as a Musical History
Material." Ongaku-gaku [Journal of the Japanese
Musicological Society] 8(3): 65-74, 1962.
Contends that The Tale of Genji, an 11th-century
novel, is valid as a historical source, and that
Murasaki Shikibu, its author, had unprejudiced and
convincing opinions on music.

816. TSUNODA Ryusaku, W. Theodore DE BARY, and Donald KEENE,
comp. Sources of Japanese Tradition. Vol.1. New
York: Columbia Univ. Press, 1958. xxiii, 506p.
Chapter 14 ("The Vocabulary of Japanese Aesthetics
II," p.277-97) contains translations of Zeami's
treatises, Yugen no saki ni iru koto ("On
Attaining the State of Yûgen") and Mannô wan
isshin no koto ("On the One Mind Linking All Pow-
ers") from the Kakyô, Kyûi shidai ("The
Nine Stages of the Nô in Order") and Shikadô-
sho ("The Book of the Way of the Highest Flower").

817. TSURUTA Kinshi and YAMAGUCHI Osamu. A Booklet of
Satsuma-Biwa. Tokyo: Kyôiku Shuppan Center,
1973. 14p.
Brief description of the Satsuma-biwa with reference to the instrument and methods of performance.

818. TUZI Jiro. "When Music Meets Tradition," Contemporary
Japan 5(3): 437-42, December 1936.
Essay concerning Japanese people's taste for
traditional and Western musics, relating the
author's personal experience.

819. TYLER, Royall. Granny Mountains: A Second Cycle of
Nô Plays. Ithaca, NY: Cornell Univ. Press, 1978.
200p.
Contains nine nô plays and five kyôgen
plays in translation.

820. _____. Pining Wind: A Cycle of Nô Plays. Ithaca,
NY: Cornell Univ. Press, 1978. 200p.
Collection of nô and kyôgen plays in
translation; contains ten nô plays and four
kyôgen.

140

\* \* \* \* \* \* \* \* \* \* \* \*

821. UCHIDA Ruriko. "The Musical Character of Rice Planting
Song in Tokunoshima Island." In Proceedings of the
Eighth International Congress of Anthropological and
Ethnological Sciences Vol.2, p.340-42, 1968.
A comparison of two types of rice planting song, one
from the Amami Islands and the other from the
Chûgoku district of mainland Japan.

822. _____. "The Musical Character of 'Taue-bayashi': A Rice
Planting Music in Japan." In Musik als Gestalt und
Erlebnis: Festschrift Walter Graf zum 65. Geburts-
tag, p.234-50. Wien: Böhlau, 1970.
Study of the taue-bayashi, a form of rice
planting music, preserved in the mountainous area of
the Chûgoku district of Japan.

823. _____. "Obriad taue-baiasi i trudovye rytmy iaponskikh
risovodov." Sovetskaia ètnografiia 1: 120-31,
1966.
On the ceremonies of taue-bayashi and the rhythm
of Japanese rice farmer's work.

824. _____. "Rice-Planting Music of Chindo (Korea) and the
Chûgoku Region (Japan)." In The Performing Arts,
Music and Dance, p.109-17. Ed. by John Blacking
and Joann W. Kealiinohomoku. The Hauge: Mouton,
1979.
Comparison of two rice-planting rituals, Korean and
Japanese, in terms of their musical, poetical, and
ethnographic characteristics.

825. _____. "Über das japanischen Volkslied." Deutsches
Jahrbuch der Musikwissenschaft für 1959: 82-92,
1960.
General remarks on Japanese folk songs and their
characteristics.

826. _____. "Die Volkslieder auf den Amami-Inseln."
Jahrbuch für musikalische Volks- und Völkerkunde
8: 47-60, 1977.
Study of the folk songs of the Amami Islands,
situated between Japan and Okinawa, dealing with
historical aspects, a classification of the folk
song types, the musical character of the songs, and

their relationships with folk song of surrounding
areas. Reprinted in a collection of the author's
essays on folk music of the Amami Islands Amami
min'yô to sono shûhen ('Amami Folksong and its
Environs'), p.275-88. Tokyo: Yûzankaku, 1983.

827. UEDA Makoto. The Old Pine Tree and Other Noh Plays.
Lincoln, NB: Univ. of Nebraska Press, 1962. xxv,
63p.
Contains translations of Oimatsu, Yashima, Higaki,
Jinen-koji, and Matsuyama-kagami.

828. UEHARA (OUEHARA) Rokushirô. "La Musique japonaise."
Revue française du Japon 2: 225-31, 1893.
Outlines the history and musical scales of Japanese
music and discusses means for regeneration of traditional music. In this lecture (given on June 17,
1893, at the meeting of the Society for the French
Language) the terms zokugaku, rio-sen [ryosen],
rissen [ritsu], yô-sen and in-sen were
introduced.

829. UMEMOTO Rikuhei. "Japanese Dancing." Transactions and
Proceedings of the Japanese Society (London) 31:
19-25, 1934.
Outline of Japanese dancing (nihon buyô),
with a description of three "formal dance" (mai)
examples: Echigo-jishi, Kanjin-cho, and
Kisen.

830. UMEMOTO Rikuhei and ISHIZAWA Yutaka. Introduction to
the Classic Dance of Japan. Tokyo: Sanseido, 1935.
32p., 82 illus.
Outline of classical Japanese dance (Nihon
buyô), touching upon its history and various
preceding dance forms, techniques, musical accompaniment, characteristics, and its spiritual nature.

831. UMEWAKA Manzaburô with F.M. KURAMOCHI. "Interview with
the Noh Actor Umewaka Manzaburô." World of
Music 17(3): 19-25, 1975.
Umewaka Manzaburô II (b.1908) talks about his
early training and gives his opinions about the
nô theater and related matters.

832. USHIYAMA Mitsuru. "Western Music in Japan."
Contemporary Japan 10(10): 1313-17, October
1941.

142

Account of the progress and popularity of Western
music in Japan up to the 1930's. Enumerates those
musicians who contributed towards this development,
including numerous performers from Europe and
America.

и  и  и  и  и  и  и  и  и  и

833. VAN ZILE, Judy. The Japanese Bon Dance in Hawaii.
Kalilua: Hawaii Press Pacifica, 1982. 96p.
General description of Japanese-Hawaii folk dancing
tradition with an emphasis on the Buddhist memorial
rites and ceremonies.

834. VEEDER, P. V. "Some Japanese Musical Intervals."
Transactions of the Asiatic Society of Japan
7(1): 76-86, 1879.
Paper read October 23rd 1878 concerning measurement
of the pitches of some "very ancient flutes and
flageolets brought from the temples at Nara,"
preceded by a long explanation of the "principles of
the physical theory of music."

* * * * * * * * * *

835. WADAGAKI Kenzô, trans. "Monoceros, the Rishi [Ikkaku
sennin]." Far East 3: 46-51, 1898.
Translation of the nô play Ikkaku sennin by
Konparu Hachirô Hata no Motoyasu.

836. _____. Stray Leaves. Tokyo, 1908. 190p.
Contains translations of Ikkaku sennin, a
nô play, and scenes from two jôruri
pieces, Kanadehon chûshingura ("Forty-Seven
Model Rônin") by Takeda Izumo, and Ichinotani
futaba gunki ("First Battle of Atsumori at
Ichinotani") by Namiki Sôsuke.

837. WADE, Bonnie C. Tegotomono: Music for the Japanese
Koto. Westport, CT: Greenwood Press, 1976. xxiv,

379p., music.
Analysis of the tegoto sections from selected
compositions of 19th-century Japanese koto
music. Includes transcriptions of five popular
koto pieces into Western notation. Based on the
author's M.A. thesis, A Selective Study of Honte-
Kaete Tegotomono in Nineteenth-Century Japanese Koto
Music, UCLA, 1967.

838. WALEY, Arthur. The Noh Plays of Japan. London:
George Allen and Unwin, 1921; Reprint ed. New York:
Grove Press, 1957.
Introduction to the nô play and translations
of 19 famous nô plays and a kyôgen play.
With summaries of 16 more nô plays.

839. WALTER, Arnold. "A Musical Journey to Japan." Canadian
Musical Journal 6: 3-12, 1962.
An account of musical life, education, and broadcasting in Japan written after a four-week trip by
the author to Japan. Contains a number of inaccuracies, but points out correctly the state of Western music in Japan at the time.

840. WATANABE Hitoshi. "The Ainu: Present Conditions of Their
Life and Urgent Needs for Field Study." Bulletin
of the International Committee on Urgent
Anthropological and Ethnological Research 8:
97-107, 1966 (Vienna).
Remarks on music and oral traditions on p.102-3.

841. WATANABE Mamoru. "Die Bühnemusik des Kabukitheaters." In
Bericht über den internationalen musikwissenschaftlichen Kongress Bonn 1970, p.605-7. Kassel:
Bärenreiter, 1971.
Brief introduction to the music of kabuki, with
a description of the role played by geza ("off-
stage") musicians in setting atmosphere.

842. WATERHOUSE, David. "An Early Illustration of the Four
Stringed Kokyû: With a Discussion on the Early
History of Japan's Only Bowed Musical Instrument."
Oriental Arts 16(2): 162-68, 1970.
Iconographical study on the origin of the ko-
kyû, and its early history.

843. _____. "Dance, Traditional." In Kodansha Encyclopedia
of Japan 2: 73-75. Tokyo: Kodansha International,

144

1983.
Short survey of the main genres of Japanese
traditional dance. Width of material covered seems
to have resulted in the inclusion of a number of
factual inaccuracies.

844. _____. "Folk Song." In Kodansha Encyclopedia of
Japan 2: 300-301. Tokyo: Kodansha International,
1983.
General survey of the characteristics of Japanese
folk song.

845. _____. "Music, Religious." In Kodansha Encyclopedia of
Japan 5: 283-84. Tokyo: Kodansha International,
1983.
Outline, with some historical treatment, of
religious music in Japan, dealing with Shintô,
Buddhist, and Christian music.

846. _____. "Music, Western." In Kodansha Encyclopedia of
Japan 5: 285-87. Tokyo: Kodansha International,
1983.
Survey of the process of introduction of Western
music into Japan after the Meiji Restoration.

847. _____. 'Religious Music.' Sub-entry (§II) of the article
"Japan." In New Grove Dictionary of Music and
Musicians 9: 506-10. Ed. by Stanley Sadie. London:
Macmillan, 1980.
Outline of the history and present status of reli-
gious music in Japan, dealing with Shintô, Bud-
dhist, and Christian music. Contains a number of
inaccuracies in regard to historical perspective.

848. _____. "Ryûkôka." In Kodansha Encyclopedia of
Japan 6: 353-55. Tokyo: Kodansha International,
1983.
Outline history of popular urban song in Japan,
concentrating on those composed after the Meiji
Restoration under the influence of Western music.

849. WATSON, Burton. "Mibu kyôgen." Japan Quarterly
6(1): 95-98,1959.
An essay in the column "Through the Eastern Window."
Field report on the kyôgen performance at Mibu
Temple of Kyoto as practiced at the time.

850. WEIPERT, H. "Das Bon-Fest." Mittheilungen der Deut-

schen Gesellschaft für Natur- und Völkerkunde
Ostasiens 8(2): 145-73, 1900.
Ethnographic study of the bon festival. Contains
15 traditional song-texts for bon dance, and
translation into German.

851. WEISGARBER, Elliot. "The Honkyoku of the Kinko-ryû:
Some Principles of Its Organization."
Ethnomusicology 12(3): 313-44, 1968.
Discussion of honkyoku, "original solo pieces,"
for shakuhachi, and transcription of three
classical compositions of the Kinko school.

852. WERDIN, Eberhard. "Betrachtungen über japanische
Musikerziehung." Musik in Unterricht 57(4):
132-36, 1966.
Remarks on the standard of Western music education
in Japan in the mid '60's, occasioned by the
author's attendance at the congress of the All Japan
Music Education Society in June 1965.

853. WERKMEISTER, Heinrich. "Impressions of Japanese Music."
Musical Quarterly 13: 100-7, 1927.
Impressionistic commentary on traditional music of
Japan and Western music in the early 20th century by
a German cellist who stayed in Japan for some 18
years.

854. WESTARP, A. "A la découverte de la musique japonaise."
Bulletin de la Société Franco-Japonaise de Paris
23-24: 61-89, 1911.
Essay consisting of three sections, which interpret
the Japanese sense of beauty in fine arts and music.
Appended by three short musical examples which re-
veal the author's interpretation of Japanese melody.

855. _____. "Japan Ahead in Music." Transactions and
Proceedings of the Japan Society (London) 10: 23-
47, 1912.
Argues that Japanese music is superior to European
music, saying "it will be far more difficult to free
the musical consciousness of Europe from the domination of harmonic unconsciousness, than to awaken the
slumbering consciousness of the delicate musical
soul of the Far East."

856. WHITEHOUSE, Wilfred, trans. "Seami Jûroku Bushû:
Seami's Sixteen Treatises." Monumenta Nipponica

4: 540-84, 1941.
See Entry 722.

857. WILSON, William R. "Two Shuramono: Ebira and
Michimori." Monumenta Nipponica 24(4): 415-
65, 1969.
Annotated translations of two nô plays from
the second (warrior) category. Introduction includes
translation and interpretation of important texts
dealing with this type of play.

858. WOLPERT, Rembrandt F. "The Five-Stringed Lute in East
Asia." Musica Asiatica 3: 97-106, 1981.
Historical remarks on the gogen-biwa, a five-
stringed lute.

859. _____. "A Ninth-Century Score for Five-Stringed Lute."
Musica Asiatica 3: 107-35, 1981.
Attempt to decipher the Gogenkinfu, at present
preserved in the Yômei Bunko (Kyoto), with a
transcription into five-line staff.

860. _____. "A Ninth-Century Sino-Japanese Lute-Tutor."
Musica Asiatica 1: 111-65.
Study of the manuscript Fushiminomiya-bon Biwa-
fu, today housed in the Archives and Mausolea
Department of the Imperial Household Agency, with

861. _____. "Tang-Music (Tôgaku) Manuscripts for Lute and
Their Interrelationships." In Music and Tradition:
Essays on Asian and Other Musics Presented to
Laurence Picken, p.69-121. Ed. by D. R. Widdess
and R. F. Wolpert. Cambridge: Cambridge Univ. Press,
1981.
Comparison of versions of 13 pieces from the tôgaku biwa repertory contained in three manuscripts, 12th century, 16th century and 19th
century, used to demonstrate the continuity of the
tradition.

862. WOLPERT, Rembrandt, Allan MARETT, Jonathan CONDIT, and
Laurence PICKEN. "'The Waves of Kokonor': A Dance-
Tune of the T'ang Dynasty." Asian Music 5(1):
3-9, 1973. (Reprinted in Gagaku Kai 52: 57-63,
1975)
Attempt to reconstruct the original melody of
Seigaiha as performed during the Heian period,

without reference to the practice of the court
musicians today.

863. WOLZ, Carl. Bugaku: Japanese Court Dance.
Providence: Asian Music Publications, 1971. 181p.
bibliog., illus., notation, glossary.
An expansion of the author's M.A. thesis at the
Univ. of Hawaii. A descriptive introduction to
bugaku, providing dance notations of basic
dance movements and of the two dances Nasori no
ha and Nasori no kyû.

864. ____. "Dance in the Noh Theatre." World of Music
17(3): 26-32. 1975.
Definition of nô dance in the context of
Japanese culture and history, and discussion of the
characteristics of nô dances. With French and
German summaries.

865. WÖSS, Margareta. "Nô, das japanische Gesamtwerk."
Österreichische Musikzeitschrift 10: 57-63,
1965.
Introduction to nô as a synthetic performing
art, and a brief description of its musical aspects.


* * * * * * * * * * *


866. YAMADA Kosçak. "The Opera 'Dawn' or 'Black Ships.'"
Contemporary Japan 9: 1432-38, November 1940.
Introduction to the opera Kurofune by its
composer, describing the circumstances of its
composition.

867. YAMAGUCHI Osamu and Richard EMMERT. "Description of the
Musical Instruments: ATPA 1976." In Asian Musics
in an Asian Perspective [Report of ATPA 1976],
p.140-252. Tokyo: Japan Foundation, 1977.
Organological description of a number of Japanese
instruments, including azusayumi, fue, kane,
kôjin-biwa, kokyû, koto, kûchô, kutû, muk-
kuri, sangen, sanshin, satsuma-biwa, shakuhachi,
and yakumo-goto.

868. YAMAMOTO Hiroko. "Characteristics of Amami Folk Songs."

148

In <u>Musical</u> <u>Voices</u> <u>of</u> <u>Asia</u> [Report of ATPA 1978],
p.131-34. Tokyo: Japan Foundation, 1980.
Detailed description of <u>Asahana-bushi</u>, a typical
folk song of the Amami Islands, and comparison of
its characteristics with those of Okinawan and
mainland Japanese folk songs.

869. YAMATO Junji. "The Place of the Person in Music
Education: A New Approach to Music Education in
Japan." <u>International</u> <u>Music</u> <u>Education</u>: <u>ISME</u> <u>Year</u>
<u>Book</u> 6: 42-48, 1979.
Discussion of the recent reform of Japanese
curriculum standards, with an examination of the
contents of the new music curriculum prepared by the
Ministry of Education, Science and Culture. Little
reference to traditional Japanese music.

870. YANO Jun'ichi. "People in the Spotlight." <u>Japan</u>
<u>Quarterly</u> 29(3): 346-50, July-September 1982.
Short article containing biographical notes on the
composer Takemitsu Tôru and the conductor Ozawa
Seiji.

871. YASUDA, Kenneth. "The Structure of <u>Hagoromo</u>, a Noh
Play." <u>Harvard</u> <u>Journal</u> <u>of</u> <u>Asiatic</u> <u>Studies</u> 33: 5-
89, 1973.
A detailed study and analysis of <u>Hagoromo</u>
followed by a complete translation of the text.
Translation includes the important addition of
technical terms for sections of the play and singing
styles.

872. YOKOI Masako. "A hagyományos japán zene [Traditional
Music of Japan]." <u>Muzsika</u> 26(9): 26-29; 26(11):
21-23, 1983; 27(2): 14-16; 27(4): 13-16, 1984
(Budapest).
Brief introduction to traditional Japanese music,
musical instruments, and notation systems.

873. YOSHIDA Gisei. "<u>Le</u> <u>Cerisier</u> <u>de</u> <u>Souma</u>: Théâtre
<u>japonais,</u> <u>drame</u> <u>en</u> <u>cinq</u> <u>actes</u> <u>et</u> <u>six</u> <u>tableaux.</u>
1898. xx, 86p.
Translation of <u>Ichi</u> <u>no</u> <u>tani</u> <u>futaba</u> <u>gunki</u>, a
<u>kabuki</u> and <u>bunraku</u> play by Namiki Sôsuke.

874. YOSHIDA Hidekazu. "Housing Japan's Avant-garde."
<u>World</u> <u>of</u> <u>Music</u> 11(3): 6-16, 1969.
Account of the founding of the Institute for

Twentieth-Century Music (Nijusseiki Ongaku Kenkyū-jo), with mention of its members, activities, and circumstances.

875. ____. Über die Musikentwicklung Japans in den letzten Hundert Jahren." In Aspekte der neuen Musik, p.97–111. Ed. by Wolfgang Burde. Kassel: Bärenreiter, 1968.
Consideration of the musical development of the past hundred years in Japan and the problems of Japanese music today. Based on a lecture given in Akademie der Künste, Berlin, in 1965.

876. YOUNG, Margaret Hershey. Japanese Kabuki Drama: The History and Meaning of the Essential Elements and of Its Theatre Art Form. Doctoral dissertation, Indiana: Indiana Univ., 1954. 397p.
Study dealing with the stage and stagecraft, actors and acting methods, dance, music, costume, make-up, plays, and playwrights of kabuki.

877. YŪDA Yoshio. "The Formation of Early Modern Jōruri." Acta Asiatica 28: 20–41, 1975.
Historical study of kinsei jōruri viewed through changes in programs, number of performers, and theatrical devices.

878. YUIZE Shin'ichi. "Means of Preservation: Preservation of Traditional Instruments." In The Preservation of Traditional Forms of the Learned Music of the Orient and the Occident, p.279–89. Ed. by W.K. Archer, Urbana, IL: Institute of Communications Research, Univ. of Illinois, 1964.
Outline history of Japanese music and description of the iemoto-seido, a system of hereditary transmission of the arts.

879. ____. "The Music of Japan." In Music—East and West: Report on 1961 Tokyo East-West Music Encounter Conference, p.15–17. Tokyo: Executive Committee of 1961 TEWMEC, 1961.
Personal views of a koto player-composer on developing a new music for traditional instruments.

\* \* \* \* \* \* \* \* \* \* \*

880. ZACHERT, Herbert and MATSUMOTO, transl. "Aoi no Ue:
Nô-Drama in zwei Akten von Komparu Ujinobu."
Monumenta Nipponica 2(2): 536-50, 1939.
German translation of the nô play Aoi no
ue, with introductory remarks concerning its
literary sources.

881. ZEDTWITZ, Freiherr von. "Japanische Musikstücke."
Mittheilungen der Deutschen Gesellschaft für
Natur- und Völkerkunde Ostasiens 4(32): 107; (33)
129-45, 1885.
Music of eight koto pieces and three naga-
uta pieces with brief commentaries. Most pieces
are taken from the Tokyo Academy of Music version.
See Entry 796.

\* \* \* \* \* \* \* \* \* \* \*

INDEXES

SUBJECT

I. Fields of Study

General Studies
87, 97, 125, 139, 150, 160, 161, 165, 168, 169, 202,
214, 236, 258, 259, 260, 261, 284, 319, 320, 358,
361, 368, 373, 391, 394, 399, 402, 434, 436, 447,
461, 469, 471, 483, 490, 493, 497, 501, 503, 519,
521, 530, 537, 542, 554, 568, 581, 586, 592, 602,
658, 660, 661, 662, 680, 703, 705, 738, 742, 745,
769, 770, 771, 772, 798, 799, 805, 811, 813, 828,
854, 855, 872, 878

Acoustics
89, 90, 209, 223, 226, 265, 617, 618, 619, 640, 690,
766, 780, 781, 782

Aesthetics
352, 434, 508, 532, 535, 608, 711, 757, 759, 760,
762, 764

Biographies
70, 72, 192, 200, 343, 403, 406, 407, 831, 870

Dance
110, 123, 124, 173, 267, 269, 280, 337, 345, 378,
423, 491, 502, 511, 607, 650, 741, 829, 830, 843,
863, 864

Disciplines
276, 285, 315, 433, 441, 536, 537, 567, 611, 613,
622, 673, 684, 697, 743

Education
84, 104, 118, 234, 334, 342, 404, 437, 456, 485,
505, 512, 555, 559, 564, 565, 574, 601, 624, 701,
704, 754, 755, 756, 767, 795, 852, 869

History
  1) General
  103, 193, 251, 273, 284, 285, 293, 294, 295, 303,
  339, 366, 483, 521, 531, 532, 556, 567, 592, 600,
  645, 658, 668, 693

  2) Prehistory to c.800 (up to Nara Period)
  112, 148, 280, 293, 322, 324, 325, 398, 439, 440,
  740, 858

  3) c.800 to c.1400 (Heian Period to Period of
     Northern and Southern Courts)
  128, 148, 177, 192, 194, 204, 215, 224, 250, 257,
  291, 293, 298, 470, 495, 506, 549, 552, 589, 629,
  634, 648, 652, 653, 656, 672, 676, 740, 815

  4) c.1400 to c.1600 (Muromachi Period)
  98, 108, 194, 305, 344, 349, 350, 414, 529, 562,
  629, 647, 702, 740

  5) c.1600 to c.1868 (Edo Period)
  70, 73, 74, 75, 76, 78, 79, 81, 88, 140, 147, 156,
  159, 186, 314, 338, 349, 384, 411, 416, 425, 430,
  465, 499, 541, 636, 637, 638, 725, 803, 877

  6) c.1868 to Present (Post-Meiji Restoration)
  115, 116, 140, 216, 217, 238, 239, 304, 310, 315,
  342, 368, 421, 425, 466, 473, 500, 564, 566, 571,
  610, 713, 716, 846

Musical Instruments
  75, 120, 121, 155, 168, 179, 183, 196, 199, 212,
  214, 223, 271, 277, 278, 283, 322, 324, 358, 396,
  420, 427, 428, 429, 439, 440, 450, 461, 518, 539,
  580, 603, 618, 619, 639, 669, 690, 728, 771, 773,
  780, 781, 782, 791, 793, 801, 809, 812, 817, 842,
  858, 859, 867

Notation
  167, 241, 250, 276, 298, 306, 323, 408, 477, 480,
  489, 534, 547, 548, 549, 551, 552, 600, 652, 653,
  654, 655, 656, 673, 684, 697, 859, 860, 861, 862,
  863

Ritual and Festival Music
  102, 127, 156, 205, 218, 224, 237, 267, 274, 280,
  288, 357, 359, 515, 516, 614, 687, 700, 706, 726,
  731, 737, 746, 845, 847, 850

Theater
    38, 107, 141, 142, 208, 262, 270, 366, 378, 410,
    418, 438, 482, 510, 583, 594, 596, 635, 668, 680,
    612, 732, 740, 800

Theory and Analysis
    69, 105, 162, 209, 211, 213, 222, 244, 251, 353,
    354, 385, 386, 388, 400, 448, 453, 455, 457, 458,
    462, 496, 499, 528, 538, 540, 586, 640, 646, 657,
    659, 669, 671, 674, 675, 698, 719, 745, 749, 750,
    751, 763, 766, 778, 785, 791, 792, 828, 834, 871

Translations of Historical Sources
    12, 109, 112, 117, 130, 143, 148, 151, 175, 187,
    194, 204, 215, 224, 257, 306, 372, 375, 390, 430,
    470, 506, 556, 598, 599, 610, 634, 637, 692, 714,
    722, 810, 816, 856

Translations and Synopses of Texts
    91, 108, 111, 114, 123, 124, 131, 132, 134, 135,
    136, 141, 143, 145, 146, 148, 149, 152, 153, 164,
    170, 175, 180, 182, 184, 206, 207, 210, 215, 220,
    221, 225, 243, 252, 263, 266, 279, 281, 289, 291,
    298, 306, 316, 317, 318, 326, 327, 328, 329, 330,
    340, 341, 344, 347, 349, 350, 355, 356, 360, 364,
    365, 367, 380, 382, 383, 412, 413, 414, 415, 417,
    444, 459, 463, 464, 465, 468, 474, 475, 476, 484,
    485, 491, 504, 509, 510, 517, 533, 544, 545, 546,
    553, 556, 562, 570, 573, 576, 577, 582, 585, 588,
    589, 590, 591, 604, 605, 609, 623, 630, 632, 642,
    643, 645, 647, 651, 663, 677, 678, 682, 683, 686,
    689, 694, 699, 700, 702, 707, 708, 709, 710, 715,
    720, 723, 729, 730, 738, 739, 779, 808, 819, 820,
    827, 835, 836, 838, 850, 857, 871, 873, 880

Vocal Style and Technique
    226, 265, 388, 438, 467, 597, 617


II. Genres of Traditional Japanese Music

Gagaku (including Bugaku, Mi-kagura, Saibara,
        Rôei and Other Court Traditions)
    92, 102, 127, 143, 148, 149, 151, 166, 167, 190,
    191, 192, 194, 195, 196, 198, 201, 203, 204, 205,
    215, 216, 217, 218, 223, 244, 245, 246, 247, 248,
    249, 250, 251, 252, 272, 282, 289, 290, 291, 292,
    293, 296, 298, 299, 301, 304, 306, 307, 308, 310,

311, 312, 322, 323, 325, 339, 362, 371, 372, 389,
397, 400, 401, 418, 423, 427, 428, 429, 432, 439,
440, 450, 460, 470, 495, 506, 511, 520, 543, 547,
548, 549, 550, 551, 552, 554, 556, 557, 583, 587,
589, 603, 607, 639, 646, 648, 652, 653, 654, 655,
656, 671, 672, 673, 674, 675, 676, 684, 699, 714,
717, 718, 719, 734, 735, 784, 785, 787, 788, 801,
815, 833, 859, 860, 861, 862, 863

Shintô Music
102, 156, 215, 218, 224, 252, 274, 280, 288, 289,
291, 298, 348, 350, 359, 401, 583, 589, 649, 676,
700, 706, 726, 845, 847

Shômyô
86, 177, 194, 226, 254, 255, 257, 287, 293, 309,
336, 405, 408, 474, 477, 614, 615

Heikyoku (Heike-biwa)
390, 444, 450, 556

Medieval Performing Arts (including Kôwakamai)
98, 100, 101, 128, 344, 347, 349, 350, 360, 556,
583, 584, 629, 634, 650, 668, 702, 731

Nô and Kyôgen
11, 101, 109, 111, 117, 118, 121, 123, 124, 127,
152, 153, 164, 171, 180, 184, 197, 203, 208, 211,
213, 221, 225, 242, 263, 264, 279, 300, 351, 352,
353, 360, 366, 377, 380, 407, 414, 415, 417, 418,
442, 463, 464, 468, 480, 481, 482, 507, 508, 511,
518, 528, 538, 544, 545, 546, 553, 562, 572, 573,
582, 583, 588, 590, 591, 594, 595, 597, 598, 604,
605, 608, 609, 617, 618, 629, 630, 631, 632, 633,
642, 643, 645, 647, 663, 667, 668, 677, 678, 679,
681, 683, 686, 689, 692, 694, 699, 713, 715, 720,
722, 723, 729, 730, 739, 741, 758, 759, 760, 761,
762, 763, 764, 765, 766, 778, 779, 783, 786, 790,
816, 819, 820, 827, 831, 835, 836, 838, 856, 857,
864, 865, 870, 880

Sôkyoku and Jiuta (Koto Music and
        Sankyoku Ensemble)
21, 70, 73, 74, 75, 76, 77, 78, 80, 81, 82, 83, 90,
158, 159, 196, 222, 237, 275, 299, 338, 343, 392,
403, 419, 422, 448, 496, 578, 601, 618, 658, 659,
661, 662, 669, 670, 696, 745, 749, 750, 796, 804,
808, 814, 837, 842, 878, 879, 881

III. Japan and the West

Early Contacts with Western Music
144, 188, 293, 305

Post-Restoration Western and Western-Influenced Music
85, 95, 115, 116, 137, 140, 163, 174, 189, 227, 229,
232, 233, 235, 266, 326, 354, 392, 395, 421, 435,
451, 485, 500, 505, 526, 564, 565, 566, 571, 575,
610, 612, 615, 620, 662, 664, 665, 691, 713, 716,
733, 768, 772, 806, 818, 832, 839, 846, 848, 853,
866, 875

Contemporary Music
85, 157, 241, 256, 331, 369, 395, 436, 451, 479,
494, 569, 616, 721, 724, 768, 784, 874, 875

Modern Musical Culture
52, 53, 138, 228, 230, 231, 253, 321, 332, 363, 377,
446, 449, 525, 559, 560, 578, 596, 620, 633, 670,
688, 774, 807, 839, 879

Japanese Music Overseas
176, 376, 563, 625, 626, 627, 628, 695, 737, 744,
833

Japanese Influence on Western Music
679, 695, 784

\* \* \* \* \* \* \* \* \* \*

NAMES
    [Co-authors, translators, persons written about, and
    others not accessible through the main alphabetization.]

\* \* \* \* \* \* \* \* \* \*

FORMAT

Collections with Staff Notation
93, 96, 119, 133, 182, 206, 207, 251, 252, 296, 316,
317, 318, 323, 355, 356, 362, 367, 374, 397, 459,
472, 476, 477, 480, 485, 488, 493, 517, 527, 533,
547, 549, 551, 552, 564, 570, 586, 606, 621, 666,
717, 727, 738, 749, 770, 796, 805, 837, 851, 854,
860, 881

Dissertations
8, 36, 70, 72, 76, 98, 103, 117, 128, 166, 186, 194,
236, 244, 251, 257, 303, 331, 335, 351, 367, 376,
409, 428, 488, 494, 533, 549, 552, 564, 574, 620,
621, 625, 629, 636, 669, 671, 679, 698, 701, 702,
726, 735, 752, 763, 783, 791, 837, 876

Encyclopedia and Dictionary Entries
71, 75, 87, 99, 106, 115, 116, 120, 168, 177, 193,
199, 200, 221, 227, 228, 229, 230, 231, 232, 233,
234, 235, 245, 246, 255, 258, 272, 274, 283, 284,
286, 287, 288, 294, 295, 299, 300, 315, 319, 346,
348, 371, 394, 395, 401, 403, 404, 405, 406, 407,
421, 434, 442, 450, 452, 454, 487, 513, 523, 524,
531, 532, 539, 631, 661, 662, 685, 712, 732, 753,
758, 775, 798, 843, 844, 845, 846, 847, 848

Items of Iconographical Importance
183, 277, 324, 469, 580, 728, 842

* * * * * * * * * *